THERE IS ONLY ONE
BAPTISM

EPHESIANS 4:4-6

Says:

THERE IS ONLY ONE BAPTISM

It Is by Full Immersion & John 3:3-5 Says:

YOU CANNOT GO TO HEAVEN WITHOUT IT

*If You Disagree, Be the First To Successfully Rebut
This Narrative Using The New Testament,*
And win $30,000
[See Appendix 1 for The Book Challenge Rules]

By

Edwin Nhliziyo Sr

B.Sc(Econ), MBA, CPA, AIB

(Auditing Church Practices in Baptism)

CITIOFBOOKS, INC.
3736 Eubank NE Suite A1
Albuquerque, NM 87111-3579
www.citiofbooks.com
Hotline: 1 (877) 389-2759
Fax: 1 (505) 930-7244

Ordering Information:
Quantity sales. Special discounts are available on quantity purchases by corporations, associations, and others. For details, contact the publisher at the address above.

Printed in the United States of America.

ISBN-13:   Paperback   979-8-90124-447-0
                  eBook   979-8-90124-448-7

TABLE OF CONTENTS

---

[1] The Expository Files www.bible.ca/ef/expository-ephesians-2-8.htm June 1997

PREVIEW

'Are you saved' '

Are you baptized?'

'Are you born again?'

'Will you go to heaven when you die?

These are among the questions that evoke so much debate and emotion in Christianity today. They are worth repeating repeatedly because they are critical to every Christian's eternal fate.

The four foundation scriptures for Christians about baptism are of course (1) *"For God so loved the world that he gave his one and only Son, that whoever <u>believes</u> in him shall not perish but have eternal life[2]"* and (2) *Whoever believes and is <u>baptized</u> will be saved, but whoever does not believe will be condemned[3]."* (3) *"<u>Therefore</u> go and make disciples of all nations, <u>baptizing</u> them in the name of the Father and of the Son and of the Holy Spirit, and teaching them to obey everything I have commanded you. And <u>surely</u> I am with you always, to the very end of the age[4]."* And (4) "Repent and be baptized, every one of you, in the name of Jesus Christ for the forgiveness of your sins. And you will receive the gift of the Holy Spirit[5]."

---

2 John 3:16
3 Mark 16:16
4 Matthew 28:19-20
5 Acts 2:38

We need to add to these verses John 3:3&5 because that's where this discussion will end up. Jesus said *"Very truly I tell you, no one can see the kingdom of God unless they are born again.* In verse 5, he said *"Very truly I tell you, no one can enter the kingdom of God unless they are born of water and the Spirit."* Let these verses be your guide, as we dig deeper into this question of baptism, and life as born-again Christians according to the New Testament.

The questions above have vexed many Christians for a very long time, and we should be putting pressure on our churches to answer these questions truthfully once and for all. That pressure should come from every Christian who was baptized, other than by full immersion. These people have been disenfranchised as born again Christians by the very churches that give them fake baptisms. According to Jesus, they cannot enter the kingdom of God, the very thing they seek.

These questions demand an answer from the Church. All Christians who have been subjected to "baptism" by pouring, sprinkling, and/or to infant baptisms need to hear that answer.

Ephesians 4:4-6 is our point of departure. It will complicate our discussion here because it tells us that *"There is one body and one Spirit, just as you were called to one hope when you were called; one Lord, one faith, **one baptism;** one God and Father of all, who is over all and through all and in all."* Our churches rarely highlight this passage in the Bible because it exposes the heart of a centuries-old deception in Christianity. It leads to the key question: If there is one baptism, which one is it and how come our churches use more than one baptism?

This book provides a conclusive answer to these questions, that is, if the Bible is what it says it is, and Jesus Christ is who he says he is, and the Christianity we are talking about is the one ushered in by the apostles on the Day of Pentecost (Acts 2:14- 41). We ask these questions in this book because they are central to every Christian's hopes and aspirations of spending eternity in heaven when they die.

Two things should be noted however, at the outset, and they both involve the apostle Paul. The first is that Christianity was almost 16 years old when the Apostle Paul wrote his first Epistle and more than 25 years old when he wrote Romans from which false prophets like to quote (Appendix IV). The second is that the apostle was writing primarily to believers in these epistles (see Galatians 5:27 ESV). It says clearly *"As many of you as were baptized into Christ have clothed yourself with Christ."* The people the apostle is addressing had not only believed in Jesus but had also obeyed his command to be baptized by full immersion. It is therefore a mistake of modern-day Christianity to use Paul's writings to re-state or modify what Jesus commanded in the Great Commission or what Peter taught on Pentecost.

On the contrary, Paul's role was to explain Jesus to both the Jews and the Gentiles, and not to reinvent him. He taught that when we are baptized, we cloth ourselves with Jesus, and that from that day forward we are included in all the promises of the Bible that come to us via the cross. We can confirm this by looking at two passages in the Bible. Romans 6:3-4 tells us we are united with Jesus Christ through baptism and Galatians 3:27 that tells us we have clothed ourselves with Jesus.

In Galatians 6:17 he went further to explain that we also bear the marks (scars of Jesus) on our bodies as well, when we are baptized. He gave similar messages in his epistles including in Acts 19:1-7 where we are told he baptized the 12 believers in Ephesus. He used the same baptism commanded by Jesus in the Great Commission when he baptized them in the name of the Lord Jesus.

Yet false prophets use his writings to try and contradict the Bible!

Whatever Paul said in his epistles was never intended to contradict or revise the teaching in Acts 2:38-39 some 25 or more years earlier. I hope Appendix IV will help someone figure this out with a clearer mind.

The primary issue in this book centers on baptism and I approach the issue from the point of view of a professional auditor. If the New Testament is our Instruction Manual as Christians, are we compliant with God's instructions? Is the Bible wrong when it says there is one baptism, but we see more than one baptism in practice. The heart of this Christian deception was the introduction of the counterfeit baptisms of pouring and sprinkling and presenting them as genuine baptisms.

It is critical to answer this question of 'one' baptism correctly in view of what Jesus said to Nicodemus in John 3:3, especially since every Christian I know wants to go to heaven when they die. He said, *"Very truly I tell you, no one can see the kingdom of God [heaven] unless they are born again."* The kingdom of God is what everybody refers to as heaven, of course. Are you going to heaven when you die, and if so, have you met the condition laid down by the Lord Jesus Christ that you should be born again?

Here, we encounter our first problem: What exactly did Jesus mean by born-again as Nicodemus asks in John 3:4? *"How can someone be born when they are old?" Nicodemus asked. "Surely they cannot enter a second time into their mother's womb to be born!"*

Nicodemus' reaction is understandable. Jesus was unclear in his statement that we should be born again. He did not define it in terms of baptism. He said instead that we should be born again of water and the Spirit.

So, what is that?

Here again, we encounter another problem in this discourse. What did Jesus mean by one being born again of water and the Spirit? The apostle Peter was left to answer that question for us on Pentecost, and later God used Philip (Acts 8:26-39) to fill in the blanks when he baptized the Ethiopian eunuch in the desert. Whatever Jesus meant must have been covered by the teaching Peter gave on Pentecost and what Philip did in the desert. Acts 2:38 ties all this together for us. If we believe and are baptized, we receive the gift of the Holy Spirit.

Most Theologians today agree that Jesus meant we should go through the Christian ritual of baptism by full immersion. To John the Baptist, baptism meant both the candidate for baptism and the baptizer stand in plentiful water [John 3:23] whereby the baptizer dunks the candidate into the water in this Christian ritual of baptism. Under the new covenant with Jesus Christ, this meant one should be dunked into water three times in the name of the Father, of the Son and of the Holy Spirit [Matthew 28:18-20]. All this was in line with the uncorrupted meaning of the verb 'to baptize', which means to dip or to immerse someone into water. It is derived from its Greek root '*baptizo*'.

That, we believe, was what the word meant to Jesus and his Apostles when they walked the earth. The Lord Jesus answered Nicodemus' question by saying *"Very truly I tell you, no one can enter the kingdom of God unless they are born (again) of water and the Spirit" (John 3:5)*. We do not know whether that answer clarified the issue for Nicodemus, but almost 21 centuries on, the debate continues about what Jesus meant. Yet when we look at the two instances of a Christian baptism in the New Testament [Matthew 3:16 and Acts 8:38-39], we know what Jesus meant from what he and his disciples did in practice. They baptized by full immersion.

So, why does confusion and uncertainty continue to reign?

The simple answer to that question is the Church, and by the Church, we are talking about the Roman Catholic Church, the only church that existed until Reformation. Church doctrine, tradition, and practice are responsible for the confusion. The Church departed from what Jesus and the apostles taught and practiced in baptism by introducing the man-made practices of pouring, sprinkling and much later on, infant baptism.

In this book, we are focusing on baptism because we want to set the record straight. I am therefore challenging the Church establishment, and the public at large, to answer my questions about baptism, and what it means for one to be born again. The term 'born-again' itself was introduced into Christianity by none other than the Lord Jesus Christ himself. There is no dispute about that. What must engage us is what he meant when he said we cannot enter the kingdom of God unless we are born again. Since every Christian's goal is to go to heaven and not end up in that other place, we should demand clarity on the issue of baptism.

So, what did Jesus mean by the term 'born again of water and the Spirit'? The Apostles who inherited Jesus' Christian ministry had no doubt what Jesus meant by baptism, or by one being born again. They knew he was talking about baptism by full immersion. That is what they practiced in their ministry, and the baptism of the Ethiopian eunuch by Philip in Acts 8:38-39 is conclusive evidence of that.

The apostles' ministry was of course the original Catholic Church, and the Church agrees that Jesus meant baptism by full immersion. We find that in paragraph 1239 of the Catechism of the Catholic Church, which says:

"Baptism properly speaking. It signifies and actually brings about death to sin and entry into the life of the Most Holy Trinity through configuration of the Paschal mystery of Christ Baptism is performed in the most expressive way by triple immersion in the baptismal water. However, from ancient times it has also been able to be conferred by pouring the water three times over the candidate's head."

There, you have it!

INTRODUCTION

When the New Testament talks about baptism, it is talking about the baptism of the Lord Jesus Christ and that of the Ethiopian eunuch. These two are the only baptisms God shows us in the whole Christian Bible, and they were both by full immersion. The Lord Jesus was baptized by John the Baptist and the eunuch by Philip, a deacon of the early Christian Church.

When we talk about the need to imitate Jesus in baptism, that is what we are talking about. We are talking about one being dipped into water in the name of God the Father, of the Son, and of the Holy Spirit as commanded by the Lord Jesus in Matthew 28:18-20. That this is the one baptism of our religion is found in Ephesians 4:4-6 where we are told there is one Baptism.

Therefore, the fact that baptism by full immersion is the only valid baptism in God's eyes comes straight from scripture, and since the eunuch's baptism took place after Pentecost, and followed the script, we know this must be the one baptism of the Christian Bible. This baptism was also done under the direction and guidance of the Spirit of God. It is therefore only logical to conclude that if there is only one baptism in Christianity, this is it. It transforms us into born again Christians. If the Church therefore were to argue that baptism by full immersion does not qualify us to enter the kingdom of God, it would be contradicting the Bible.

That becomes our first challenge question. If the Bible says there is only one baptism, how do we explain the many baptisms in the Christian

Church today? If therefore your Church, your Pastor, or anyone else is telling you you're baptized when you have not been baptized by full immersion, chances are they are misleading you, and this book is meant for you. It is a call to action. If they are telling you; you have been baptized after pouring water on you, sprinkling water on you, or that you were baptized as a baby, they are deceiving you. If they are telling you, you're saved through grace alone through faith in Jesus (Ephesians 2:8-9), they are misleading you. Simply stated, if you have not been baptized by full immersion, sometimes referred to as imitating Jesus in baptism, you need to wake up, Child of God, and take control of your own eternity.

You do that by studying the Bible and focusing first and foremost on John 3:3 and John 3:5 and what they mean to you or should mean to you. Your goal is to answer the one question: What did Jesus mean by one being born again. Decide for yourself where the truth lies and this book is a good starting point in that process. It is not meant to be comprehensive. It simply lays down the foundation upon which you should build your Christianity.

The key message of this book is that all the blessings of the New Testament come to you through Jesus's ultimate sacrifice on the cross, and that anyone who has not been united with Jesus Christ through baptism is not included. My authority for saying that is Romans 6:3-4 that says *"Or don't you know that all of us who were baptized into Christ Jesus were baptized into his death? We were therefore buried with him through baptism into death in order that, just as Christ was raised from the dead through the glory of the Father, we too may live a new life."* Scripture does not lie.

Throughout this book, I will offer you verses from the Bible to guide you. For example, Jesus told us in Matthew 7:15 to *"Watch out for false prophets. They come to you in sheep's clothing, but inwardly they are ferocious wolves."* False prophets are still among us. They will mislead you about baptism and other things in Christianity. Be wary of them, and some of them are hiding in plain sight, right there in front of you, in your church's own pulpit. These people will rewrite the word of God to serve their own selfish purposes. Some of them do it because they are themselves ignorant, parroting whatever they were taught at seminary without analyzing it.

Ask yourself the question, who might these people Jesus was talking about be today? In Matthew 23:13 Jesus identified them in his own time. He said of them, *Woe to you, teachers of the law and Pharisees, you hypocrites! You shut the door of the kingdom of heaven in people's faces. You yourselves do not enter, nor will you let those enter who are trying to."* He was talking about today's clergy, including the Christian charlatans who help propagate these lies and practices. Jesus also told us about the possible impact of their falsehoods on our own eternity. He said they shut the door to heaven of people like you and me who genuinely want to go to heaven.

As I said before, these people still exist today. They are your church leaders, the clergy, the academics, Christian bloggers, and social media influencers who reinforce falsehoods about baptism every chance they get. They will tell you that when they pour and sprinkle water over you, you have been baptized. But that is not what the Bible says, is it? As we have seen, the Bible says there is one baptism, and that one baptism cannot be different from what John the Baptist, and Jesus and the apostles practiced.

Some of these false prophets will go as far as telling believers that grace alone through faith in Jesus Christ saved them. This comes from Ephesians 2:8-9 that says, "For it is by grace you have been saved, through faith—and this is not from yourselves, it is the gift of God— not by works, so that no one can boast." However, that 'save' in Ephesians 2:8-9 is not the same 'save' as the one we find in Mark 16:16 for example. The message in Ephesians 2:8-9 is to believers who have already been baptized by full immersion. That's why the Apostle says what he says in his Epistle to the Ephesians. They have been saved (already) by grace through faith.

These people are already saved through baptism, and they demonstrated their faith in Jesus by being baptized. Now this concept of faith and baptism can be confusing, and to help you understand what it involves, I have included an article by Steve Dewhirst on the subject as Appendix II. It is an admission that I can never explain the underling concepts of faith and obedience in the Great Commission better than Mr. Dewhirst.

What Paul is saying here does not apply to you if you have not been baptized by full immersion. If you doubt my words here, go back and read Romans 6:3-4 and ask yourself the same question: Who is the apostle Paul talking to here? He is talking to believers who have been united with Jesus through baptism, and he says it plainly in that verse. Our gateway to partaking in the saving grace that comes to us via the cross is baptism and the best way to determine if you have been misled by the false prophet about baptism, is to ask yourself if Acts 2:38 and Romans 6:3-4 apply to you. They should apply to every Christian who has been baptized by full immersion.

Now look at John 3:3-5 again and ask yourself this one question – who is blocking me from entering the kingdom of heaven if it all comes down to baptism by full immersion. Isn't it the pastor who gave you a counterfeit baptism when you asked to be baptized? Isn't it your Church that teaches you falsely that one is saved by grace alone through faith alone? What about the blogger and the academic who join to perpetuate these falsehoods?

I will expose some of these groups as I document their activities throughout this book. If they want to defend themselves, let them enter my $30,000 Book Challenge and submit a rebuttal of all the points I have laid out in Appendix 1 to this book. One of them is that there is no such thing as faith in Jesus without baptism by full immersion. Rebut this statement if you can. Likewise, there is no 'saving grace' without a proper baptism, and the blood of Jesus does nothing for you if you have not been baptized by full immersion(Appendix IV).

If you agree with me that it is the clergy, which includes your pastor, your bishop, your archbishop, your Pope, etc., who are misleading you about baptism, then Jesus is talking to you in Matthew 23:13 that I quoted above. You're the one who is being prevented from entering the kingdom of God by the false teachings of the Church and its agents.

You're the one who is the victim of these lies.

The other day, I came across something on Concordia University's website that caught my attention. It was about grace alone, faith alone that represents a good example of this abuse of scripture by even some places of higher learning. They are part of today's Pharisees and Sadducees that Jesus rebuked in the Bible. I ask Concordia University to answer the question who the Apostle was talking to in Romans 6:3-4 and Galatians 2:8-9. Was he not talking to believers who had already been baptized by full immersion? How can you quote this passage and pretend it also applies to the unbaptized?

If your issue is that you do not know which baptism the Bible is talking about, Matthew 3:16-17 (baptism of Jesus Christ) and Acts 8:38-39 (baptism of the Ethiopian eunuch) should be your guide. They both went into the water and came up from the water when their baptism was complete. Acts 2:26-38 (St. Peter on the day of Pentecost) tells us everything else we need to know about what it means to be baptized into Christ. It is a baptism that transforms us into new creations in Jesus Christ. The Apostle Paul says in 2 Corinthians 5:17, *"Therefore, if anyone is in Christ, the new creation has come: The old has gone, the new is here!"* To be in Christ means you have been baptized by full immersion, and this newness comes solely from your baptism.

We are also told that our [old] sins are washed away, and we receive the gift of the Holy Spirit. Our new sins are also forgiven, but only if we ask God for forgiveness. 1 John 1:9 assures us that once we are 'in Christ' *"If we confess our sins, he [God] is faithful and just and will forgive us our sins and purify us from all unrighteousness."* The confusion that allows false prophets to roam free from the pulpit stems from the use of the word 'saved' in the Bible. If you believe in Jesus, you are saved, but this 'saved' is just the beginning of your journey to salvation. Mark 16:16 tells us once we believe we should be baptized to be saved. Acts 2:38 confirms that message, but it does not end there, the same Jesus also tells us that 'only those who endure to the end will be saved[6].

I encourage every reader to read or listen to the whole chapter for context every time I reference a verse in order to grasp what these verses really mean. We know that after this simple Christian ritual called baptism, we are entitled to all the 6 Matthew 24:13 promises of the Bible that f low to us through God's grace from Jesus's ultimate sacrifice on the cross. Do these same blessings f low to people who have not been baptized?

The Bible does not say so.

A major benefit that comes to you as a born-again Christian is of course the promise of the forgiveness of sins quoted above. Other people refer to this promise as a "Get Out of Jail Free" card as in the game of Monopoly. I happen to agree. The assurance above however comes with a limitation. Hebrews 10:26-27 says, *"If we deliberately keep on sinning after we have received the knowledge of the truth, no sacrifice for sins is left, but only a fearful expectation of judgment and of raging fire that will consume the enemies of God."* This verse puts the lie in those who preach the 'once saved, always saved' message.

I will not pretend here to know how Hebrews 10:26-27 operates in our daily lives. Neither do I pretend to know when this verse is triggered in a born-again believer's life. My guess however is that if you continue to live in sin, after you come to realize that you're offending against God, there comes a time when the blood of Jesus will stop working for you, unless you change your ways.

Within the context of this verse however, one must wonder how God deals with involuntary sins such as anger, lying, lust, etc., things that are triggered in us at a very subconscious level. True Christians confess these sins in their daily prayers and ask God to forgive them. However,

---

6 Matthew 24:13

if you're in the habit of raiding your neighbor's wife or husband, confessions like this without repentance will not work until you stop.

CHAPTER 1

Did Jesus Baptize?

After this, Jesus and his disciples went out into the Judean countryside,
where he spent some time with them, and baptized.

John 3:22

We set the stage for our discussion by asking a simple question: Did Jesus baptize anyone? John 3:22 answers that question conclusively when it says *"After this* [Jesus's own baptism by John the Baptist], *Jesus and his disciples went out into the Judean countryside, where he spent some time with them, and baptized*[7]*."* From this verse, it would seem, if Jesus baptized at all as scripture says, he would have baptized his disciples or at least some of them first. There is no record of John the Baptist baptizing any of Jesus' disciples.

Now, if the Bible is clear that Jesus baptized, why do we encounter so many articles on the Internet and elsewhere claiming that Jesus did not baptize anyone? That is a tough question to answer, and it is even harder for the uninitiated. The reasons behind that narrative are hard to fathom. One suspects however that the false prophets of our Christian world are afraid that if they concede the truth that Jesus baptized, then they would also have to admit that he baptized by full immersion. That then would force them to admit that this must be the same baptism he commanded in the Great Commission (Matthew 28:19-20).

---

[7] John 3:22

The trigger for this discussion is of course Ephesians 4:4-6 that says there is one baptism. Unfortunately, that is the one thing organized Christianity is determined to hide from you. Searching the Internet, I came across many articles making the argument that Jesus did not baptize anyone, despite what the Bible says. I found one written for the Progress-Index by a Dr. Lovorn particularly provoking. In it, Dr. Lovorn claimed that Jesus did not baptize anyone himself and here is how this pastor chose to distort scripture. He says "*After this, the Apostle wrote in John 3:22 that Jesus baptized. However, he corrected himself in John 4:2 to say that Jesus didn't baptize, but his disciples did. So, these verses indicate that Jesus taught his disciples how to baptize, but he didn't baptize anyone himself.*"

The pastor's statement leaves us with an unanswered question however: - if Jesus did not baptize anyone, who baptized his disciples? The statement by Pastor Lovorn is of course a complete distortion of the truth, and it is easy to see why he is wrong. In John 3:22 quoted above, which could have been written before John 4:1-2, the Apostle makes a clear statement that Jesus baptized. Remember here that the apostle John was witness to what Jesus did in the Judean countryside. That should provide us with a clear answer to the question 'did Jesus baptize anyone?' But the Church and its agents are uncomfortable with any narrative that says Jesus baptized. Otherwise, why would pastors like Dr. Lovorn try to revise the statement in John 3:22 to say what it did not say?

My guess is the apostate church that emerged as the Roman Catholic Church after Constantine took over the original Catholic Church early in the 4th century needed to deemphasize the critical role baptism by full immersion plays in our transformation. They were now admitting unbaptized pagans into the Church, including Constantine the Great himself. Asking them to submit to baptism by full immersion was too much of a stretch. After all, their primary goal was to integrate Constantine's pagan religious order into the Catholic Church, not necessarily to uphold the Bible.

Furthermore, the Catholic Church's new puppet master, Constantine the Great, was himself not baptized. He therefore might not have approved of the Church forcing baptism on members of his pagan religious order. Recall that Constantine himself was a Christian only in name throughout his more than 20-year reign. He was never baptized. History records only that he was baptized on his deathbed, which leaves us to conclude he must have been baptized by pouring or sprinkling. I say that because it is hard to imagine anyone being dunked into water while on their death bed.

So, according to my reading of the Bible on baptism, Constantine was never baptized. Even based on the wording on baptism found in the Catechism of the Catholic Church, Constantine did not receive a proper baptism, which can only be conferred by triple immersion in water. So, he died a pagan.

Over the centuries however, pouring as a way of baptizing the converted became the norm in the Church. In fact, with time, the Church dispensed with baptism by full immersion altogether, and for some 13 centuries, that remained the status quo. To this day therefore, while the Church pays lip service to baptism by full immersion in its Catechism, it continues to use pouring and/or sprinkling to baptize believers.

A challenge question here is therefore: *Does pouring, sprinkling or infant baptisms baptize, biblically?* By baptize in this sense I mean, does pouring, sprinkling or infant baptism bring about the same spiritual benefits/blessings of the forgiveness of sins and the indwelling of the Holy Spirit that allows Christians to partake in God's saving grace. We know baptism by full immersion does. Does pouring or sprinkling allow us to partake in all the promises of the New Testament that come to Christians via the cross? The answer to this question should be no, especially in view of the apostle Paul's epistles that emphasize the need for baptism that unites us with Jesus and the cross. If this is so, why does the Church claim otherwise?

It seems, the Church needed a narrative for its new doctrine that was then evolving to accommodate pagan practices brought into the Church by Constantine. Despite all these developments in the early church under Constantine, the Bible truth that Jesus baptized, and that baptism is by full immersion remains. Scripture is clear and confirms that Jesus baptized as this other passage, from the same gospel of John, recorded.

"Now John also was baptizing at Aenon near Salim, because there was plenty of water, and people were coming and being baptized. (This was before John was put in prison.) An argument developed between some of John's disciples and a certain Jew over the matter of ceremonial washing. They came to John and said to him, "Rabbi, that man who was with you on the other side of the Jordan—the one you testified about—look, he is baptizing, and everyone is going to him. To this John replied, "A person can receive only what is given them from heaven. You yourselves can testify that I said, 'I am not the Messiah but am sent ahead of him.' The bride belongs to the bridegroom. The friend who attends the bridegroom waits and listens for him and is full of joy when he hears the bridegroom's voice. That joy is mine, and it is now complete. He must become greater; I must become less.[8]

This is a second time we are told Jesus baptized, but scripture like this is never enough for these false prophets. They simply go elsewhere in the Bible to find another passage that can be used to support their preferred narrative. Typically, they will not focus on passages that undermine their narrative, and as it turns out, it is not difficult to find verses that can be abused and manipulated to undermine scripture. I wrote about these abuses in my other book Christian Satanic Verses. That book explains what these satanic verses are and suggests they are of the antichrist. Christians will take a verse and distort its true meaning to mislead the f lock.

I then ask the question if these satanic verses are not devil inspired.

Typically, they distort the true meaning of a verse to mislead you and me.

---

8 John 3:23-30p'

Unfortunately, this will continue to be our experience as Christians, as long as nobody holds the Church's feet to the fire. They will cite passages that deemphasize baptism, usually without context, to make their point that a water baptism is not required or necessary for salvation.

I am aware that one of the world's most respected Evangelists, the Reverend Billy Graham also held this mistaken view, but to his credit, he made sure he joined the "Jesus Club" by imitating Jesus in baptism. By that I mean that he made sure that like Jesus, he too was baptized by full immersion. About him we can say with confidence that he made it to heaven (John 3:3), and like everyone else, he also awaits judgment day.

To disagree with my statement above is to make Jesus a liar, for he told us we cannot enter the kingdom of God without being born again of water and the Spirit. If by this Jesus meant baptism by full immersion, Billy Graham qualified to enter the kingdom of God. In all his evangelical events, he never failed to urge others, the converted, I mean, to look for a Bible-believing church and get baptized. He was however aware of the existence of counterfeit baptisms in the Church but chose not to confront the issue directly.

So, what is Baptism exactly?

Christian baptism is defined by what Jesus has shown us. He defined it by what John the Baptist did, when he baptized him. He went into the water with him and immersed him in the water. It is defined by what Jesus himself must have done when he baptized in the Judean countryside and taught his disciples how to baptize. It is defined by what Jesus's own disciples did in their ministry, which cannot be different from what they were taught, and what they did when *Philip baptized the Ethiopian eunuch in Acts 8:38-39. The Bible says "And he [the eunuch] commanded the chariot to stand still: and they went down both into the water, both Philip and the eunuch; and he baptized him. And when they were come up out of the water, the Spirit of the Lord caught away Philip, that the eunuch saw him no more, and he [the eunuch] went on his way rejoicing."*

This definition of baptism is consistent with the original definition of its Greek root, '*baptizo*' in Jesus' time. It meant to dip or immerse into water. 'Modern day dictionaries now contradict the Bible by including in their definitions of baptism man-made practices in baptism such as pouring, sprinkling and infant baptism that did not exist when Jesus walked the earth, and therefore may be counterfeit.

In my research, I came across these two definitions among others, of the verb to baptize. The first was 'to dip in water or sprinkle water on as a part of the ceremony of receiving into the Christian community.' The second one said simply 'a Christian sacrament marked by ritual use of water and admitting the recipient to the Christian community.' Others included 'pouring water' as part of this Christian ritual or sacrament. It is clear these definitions have been corrupted to include man-made practices in baptism that are potentially fake.

We know Jesus was baptized in the River Jordan by full immersion, so there is no dispute there. The Bible does not show us the Lord Jesus Christ baptizing anyone, but it tells us about the Lord Jesus baptizing. As I pointed out above, that omission has allowed some Christians to ask the question: Did Jesus himself baptize anyone?

I have already shown that the Bible answers that question for us. Yes, Jesus baptized, and I am sure anyone who seriously reads the Bible knows the truth that Jesus baptized. We can also look at another Bible verse that tells us *"Jesus learned that the Pharisees had heard that he was gaining and baptizing more disciples than John— although in fact it was not Jesus who baptized, but his disciples.*[9]*"* This passage records what the Pharisees heard. What they heard might not have been accurate, but that is what they heard. Now, notice that last part of the verse that says Jesus himself was not the one who baptized, but that it was his disciples who did. That has been taken out of context and exploited by the false prophets to distort the truth about Jesus and baptism in many articles I have come across on the subject. As I pointed out above, this abuse

---

9 John 4:1

of Bible verses sometimes goes as far as suggesting that Jesus did not himself baptize anyone.

The Bible says no such thing.

The context here was that 'Jesus was baptizing more people than John the Baptist' but that it was not Jesus alone versus John the Baptist, but rather, Jesus plus his 12 disciples versus John the Baptist. In other words, Jesus was probably baptizing less than John on a one-to-one basis, but Jesus plus his disciples together were baptizing more than John.

That is what I believe the passage is saying. But Christian charlatans interested only in downplaying the critical importance of baptism by full immersion in our transformation into Christians, make this and similar arguments to mislead believers.

If John 3:3-3 is about going to heaven, then the churches that are engaged in this activity are preventing their followers from going to heaven. That is how Christians who have not been baptized by full immersion should view their predicament. They are being prevented from entering the kingdom of God by their own pastors. The only one who stands to benefit from such disinformation is the devil himself.

The Bible tells us in 2 Thessalonians 2:4 that the devil "... *will oppose and will exalt himself over everything that is called God or is worshiped, so that he sets himself up in God's temple,* proclaiming himself to be God." Is it possible that it is the devil who is behind this confusion in the Christian Church? Let us remember in this connection that Jesus saw this coming and warned us when he said about the Pharisees and teachers of the law, *"Woe to you, teachers of the law and Pharisees, you hypocrites! You shut the door of the kingdom of heaven in people's faces. You yourselves do not enter, nor will you let those enter who are trying to*[10]*."*

If therefore you're a Christian reading this, you owe it to yourself not to become a victim of the disinformation by the Church on this issue. You need to do the necessary due diligence and take the necessary

---

10 Matthews 23:13

corrective action. If John 3:3-5 is about baptism by full immersion and you get it wrong, you will not get a second chance. To the churches that use potentially fake baptisms, my question has always been: What will happen to these people you are deceiving when they die and God does not accept pouring, sprinkling, infant baptism and other practices we find in our churches today. If they cannot go to heaven, where do they end up?

Some churches are honest about this. Pentecostals baptize by full immersion. The Salvation Army on the other hand does not baptize at all, despite the visible charity work they do in our communities. They however do not discourage their members from getting baptized in churches that baptize. Even though on the surface they appear to be the biggest offenders of the command by the Lord Jesus to baptize the converted, they are honest and therefore do not deceive anyone.

Before we condemn the false prophets for all these practices however, we need to acknowledge that most are themselves victims of their own religious training and ignorance. They have been brainwashed into reading the Bible in a certain way. On baptism, Bible commentaries are part of the problem. They too appear to be in on this 'Jesus did not baptize anyone' bandwagon despite the Bible saying otherwise.

We will tackle that subject in the next chapter.

CHAPTER 2

Jesus, Believing, Baptism and Obedience

Watch out for false prophets. They come to you in sheep's clothing, but inwardly they are ferocious wolves.

Matthew 7:15

Before we leave the subject of whether Jesus baptized or not, let us take some time to ponder some imponderables in Christianity. Bible Commentaries do not have the authority of the Bible. They are however a great source of information about our religion.

On baptism and the question whether Jesus baptized anyone, they tend to agree with the false prophets. They tend to peddle the Jesus did not baptize falsehoods. For example, Gill's Commentary 'dances' around the issue whether Jesus baptized anyone in a very intriguing but revealing way. It only allows for the truth that Jesus baptized indirectly by quoting someone else as follows: *"The Persic version indeed suggests, as if both Christ and his disciples baptized, rendering the words thus, "Jesus was not alone who baptized, but the disciples also baptized": whereas the truth of the matter is, that Christ did not baptize in water at all: but his disciples; they baptized in his name, and by his orders, such who were first made disciples by him."*

The first question we should ask is, if Jesus did not baptize at all, who baptized the disciples. There is no record of John the Baptist baptizing any of the disciples, which can only lead us to the one possible conclusion, and that is, Jesus must have baptized them. While the point 'who baptized the disciples is not covered by scripture, it is a safe assumption to make that Jesus must have baptized at least one of them given what we already know, that after his own baptism, Jesus withdrew into the Judean countryside where he baptized. That Jesus baptized is a fact, factually recorded by someone who was present and was probably baptized by Jesus or was taught how to baptize by Jesus. It is not a figment of someone's own imagination.

The assumption has always been that Jesus would have baptized his disciples first before he let them baptize believers. In fact, for the disciples to be able to baptize, they must themselves have been baptized. These Bible Commentaries however do not see it that way. They tend to use that last line in John 4:2, just as Dr. Lovorn did, to claim that it was a correction of John 3:22. They use the verse that says *although in fact it was not Jesus who baptized, but his disciples*[11]" to support their view that Jesus did not baptize at all. According to some of these folks, the apostle John was in the habit of putting things in brackets in his writings, and this was one of those situations.

Fair, enough, but why suggest here that his statement in John 4:2 was a correction or that it modified his previous statement in John 3:22 which was factual, as Dr. Lovorn does? The apostle in 3:22 made a factual statement about a situation in which he was an active participant. He never retracted that statement. It is logical that if Jesus withdrew to the Judean countryside with his disciples and baptized, his disciples would be the first to be baptized. He taught them to baptize by baptizing at least one of them, if not all of them.

Context is important here. John 3:22 tells us what Jesus did after his baptism in the River Jordan. There is nothing to correct there. John 4:1-2 on the other hand, tells us about what the Pharisees heard. They heard that Jesus was baptizing more than John. That was not totally accurate because Jesus was baptizing along with his 12 disciples. The part in parenthesis in John 4:2, if it is a correction at all, it is a correction

---

11 John 4:2

of what the Pharisees heard. They heard that Jesus was baptizing more than John, which was not correct. The apostle is not correcting his factual statement in John 3:22. There was nothing to correct there. It is a correction of what the Pharisees thought they heard or heard.

While the Bible does not explicitly tell us who baptized the disciples, one would assume that Jesus's first order of business when he withdrew to the Judean countryside was to baptize his disciples. We know in the case of the Apostle Paul, Ananias baptized him. It was necessary for him to be baptized before embarking on his Christian journey. The same would have been expected of the Twelve.

With this information now in the record, we can ask why the discourse about Jesus not baptizing is necessary at all when scripture is so clear on the subject. This is not something I can explain, but it begs an answer. Those making these arguments should be the ones to explain the basis of their claim that Jesus did not baptize.

I have already commented above about Bible Commentaries in general. They tend to go the same direction as Dr. Lovorn. He is therefore not alone. He is part of a much larger group in the Christian community who sow confusion and doubt about Jesus, baptism, faith, and obedience. Appendix II to this book is an article by Steve Dewhirst that tries to explain these foundational Christian principles around baptism. I include this material in my book as a concession to the reality that I could never explain these principles any better myself than he does.

Yet false prophets continue to play around with scripture to spin a story designed only to mislead believers. The problem is that none of us can quite figure out why they are distorting scripture. The Bible says God is Spirit and that we should worship him in spirit and in truth. Where is that truth here?

Does this make these people and organizations Christian charlatans? I am not qualified to judge them, but I am interested in an open discussion on these matters. That is why I am inviting them to counter my argument, to defend themselves if indeed there is a defense. I have offered a prize for anyone who can prove me wrong, and the challenge is open to everyone. If the prize remains unclaimed in 12 months, I will accept victory, and so will many of the victims of these man-made practices in baptism. As I pointed out above, it seems the Church and its agents desperately want us to believe that Jesus never baptized anyone as part of a narrative that water baptism is not necessary for salvation. That narrative somehow fits in with church practices today. These people fail to realize that there can be no genuine Christianity without baptism by the one baptism of the Christian Bible, that is if the Great Commission is the center piece of Jesus' message to his church before he ascended to heaven.

Given that the Bible does not contradict itself, if there is one baptism in Christianity, it follows that without that one baptism, the cross does not benefit those who have not received it. The Bible tells us we need to be united with the Lord Jesus Christ through baptism for the cross, i.e., the blood of Jesus to work for us. That is the explicit message of Romans 6:3-4 that says, *"Or don't you know that all of us who were baptized into Christ Jesus were baptized into his death? We were therefore buried with him through baptism into death in order that, just as Christ was raised from the dead through the glory of the Father, we too may live a new life."*

Since holding the view that Jesus must have baptized his apostles is consistent with the known facts and does not contradict the Bible, we can safely make that assumption until new evidence to the contrary emerges. This is one of the points contestants in my $30,000 Book Challenge must address. Arguing that the Bible is silent on the question is not an acceptable answer because John 3:22 is clear and unambiguous.

These people make the same false claims concerning the Apostle Paul of course. He said in 1 Corinthians 1:17 *"For Christ did not send me to baptize, but to preach the gospel—not with wisdom and eloquence, lest the cross of Christ be emptied of its power."*

Many of these Christian writers will abuse this verse to imply that the Apostle Paul himself did not baptize anyone. The truth is he baptized, and he even names, names. What he was saying in the above-quoted verse is that evangelism was what God sent him to do and that the task of baptizing believers was something he could delegate to others. Once people heard and believed the story of Jesus, being baptized was simply an act of obedience (Mark 16:16 and Matthew 28:19-20).

It was Jesus himself who joined believing in Jesus, baptism and obedience together in Matthew 28:19-20. In short, believing and baptism are a command that should be obeyed. Apostle Peter repeats the same message in Acts 2:38. He said those who believe the good news should repent and be baptized. He also told us when we obey this command we will receive the gift of the Holy Spirit. Baptism is therefore about obedience to Jesus' instructions in the Great Commission.

We should also not lose sight of the fact that Acts 2:38 was an answer to a question from the Jews who witnessed Pentecost. The question they asked Peter and the other apostles, was "Brothers, what shall we do?" What he said was they should believe (which they already did) and be baptized (in obedience to Jesus' instructions in the Great Commission), and that when they do that, they will get the gift of the Holy Spirit.

As for the Apostle Paul, proof that he baptized is there in the Bible. In Acts 19:1-7, we are told Paul baptized 12 disciples in Ephesus in the name of Jesus Christ and that the Holy Spirit came on them, and they spoke in tongues and prophesied. Paul also admits to baptizing Crispus and Gaius and one other (Stephanas) in 1 Corinthians 1:14-17. So, what better evidence do these charlatans need to get their facts straight? We can also look at this issue within the context of the Great Commission.

Evangelism and baptizing the converted were commanded by the Lord Jesus Christ. The only question to ask ourselves should be which baptism did the Lord Jesus Christ command? I answer that question in the next Chapter. I need to point out at the outset however that this baptism must have been the same baptism Jesus taught his disciples.

This same baptism is repeated in Acts 8:38-39 where Philip uses it to baptize the Ethiopian eunuch. That must be the baptism Jesus commanded his disciples to use when he told them. *"Go therefore and make disciples of all nations, baptizing them in the name of the Father and the Son and the Holy Spirit, teaching them to obey everything I have commanded you. And surely I am with you always, to the very end of the age.[12]"*

We also know that baptism was by full immersion because (1) that was the meaning of the Greek root of the word 'baptizo' (to baptize) in Jesus' time, and (2) in both Jesus' baptism and the eunuch's baptism, the words "when they came out of the water' are repeated, confirming to us that both the candidate for baptism and his baptizer were in water during the act of baptism. When we imitate Jesus in baptism, we are essentially doing the same thing.

Should we be surprised that there are people in the Church trying to block us from entering the kingdom of God by misleading us about baptism? Not at all. As I said above, the Lord Jesus saw this coming and warned us about these church leaders. That is why the Church today promotes counterfeit practices such as pouring, sprinkling, and the so-called infant baptisms, and presents them as the same thing as baptism by full immersion. By so doing, they implicitly make the false claim that their counterfeit baptisms confer on the believer the same spiritual benefits and blessings as baptism by full immersion.

It is therefore worth highlighting that certain benefits that come to us by way of the cross require that we receive the baptism of the New Testament first. Greatest among the promised benefits are (1) the forgiveness of sins (Acts 2:38; 1 John 1:9; (2) the indwelling of the Holy Spirit (Acts 2:38) and (3) the grace that comes to us via the cross. Two verses about grace are appropriate here. John 1:16-17 says, *"Out of his fullness we have all received grace in place of grace already given. For the law was given through Moses; grace and truth came through Jesus Christ."* This confirms the reality that there was grace before Jesus, and that

---

12 Matthew 2o:19-20

through him we received additional grace. This is the grace I like to call "Christian grace" because it comes to us via the cross.

Romans 6:14 states, *"For sin shall no longer be your master, because you are not under the law, but under grace."* The verse contrasts mosaic law with the new covenant with

Jesus. The Jews remained under mosaic law while Christians crossed over to the new covenant with Jesus. The verse does not say we will sin no more after our baptism, but that sin will no longer control us. What moved us from being under the law to being under grace is not what happened on the cross, but what we did when we embraced Jesus by believing and being baptized (Mark 16:16).

We can therefore ask a general question of these false prophets: *If these churches and pastors are not leading us to the kingdom of God through baptism (reference John 3:3-5 here), where exactly are they leading us?* According to scripture, there are only two places one can go when they die – they either go to heaven or they go to hell. So, if the Church is not leading us to heaven, it must be pretty obvious where they are leading us – it is leading us to hell. But why?

Now we may ask another general question: what is the mission of these churches that do not baptize by full immersion. Are they on a *secret mission to mislead the flock, and if so, on whose side are these churches on?* Clearly not on God's side!

We need to also admit the obvious though, our ignorance of scripture knows no bounds, and this is part of the problem. Christians carry the Bible, but do not really read it. They do not even take advantage of the audio Bibles that are now available everywhere to at least listen to scripture. This has helped those masquerading as angels of light in our midst to succeed. The Bible tells us about them.

In Matthew 7:15 we are told to *"Watch out for false prophets. They come to you in sheep's clothing, but inwards they are ferocious wolves."* This verse repeats the same message in 2 Corinthians 11:14 where the Bible says, *"And no wonder, for even Satan disguises himself as an angel of Light."*

These are serious allegations to make against the Church, and we therefore need the Church to step forward and defend itself. I believe that this is part of the deception we are fighting against. We can fight back by studying our Bibles. If reading is a problem for you, turn on the Audio Bible and listen, even while you are doing your daily chores; things like cooking, cleaning, riding the bus or train and the like. You can also listen to the Bible while driving to and from work.

We also need to ask why our clergy is lying to us about baptism? There surely must be a good reason behind this. Most of these people are very educated people biblically. They are very knowledgeable about the Bible. So, they know everything I know and more. Some spent years in seminary school. Why then are they perpetuating a lie, and doing it in the name of the Lord Jesus Christ? It is as if they know what their audience wants to hear, and they are simply singing to the choir.

There is also something that looks like this growing tendency, especially in politics today, that if one repeats a lie over and over, people will start to believe it. That is exactly what has happened in Christianity as well. Their goal as a group, is to support their false narrative that a water baptism is not transformative and therefore not necessary for salvation. They need to maintain that position to keep all the Christians they have given a counterfeit baptism to, in line.

That could explain why they continue to say and preach a lie about baptism despite what scripture says.

CHAPTER 3

WHICH BAPTISM

"There is one body and one Spirit, just as you were called to one hope when you were called; one Lord, one faith, one baptism; one God and Father of all, who is over all and through all and in all."

Ephesians 4:4-6

Jesus, whom all Christians claim to follow was baptized in the River Jordan by full immersion. Every Christian agrees he is our example. It is not surprising therefore that when we ask Christians whether they have been baptized, the quick answer we get is 'Yes'. This answer is not based on them having imitated Jesus in baptism, but in church practices in baptism.

The correct answer to this question depends on the type of baptism the person received. Most of our churches baptize, yes, but many of our established churches use counterfeit man-made baptisms. The Bible is clear that there is only one baptism in Christianity (Ephesians 4:4-6). It is therefore when we ask a follow-up question – which baptism did you receive, that we get a clearer picture.

We are trying to determine if these people who claim to be baptized have all imitated Jesus in baptism. If the Bible says there is one baptism, anyone who has not received that baptism is not baptized? Imitating Jesus in baptism means that one has been baptized by full immersion, just as Jesus was, and just as the Ethiopian eunuch was. It is therefore only when we ask these questions that we begin to appreciate the full extent of the deception we have been subjected to by some of our churches.

The biggest group of people who have been deceived by the church are those who were baptized by pouring, sprinkling or were baptized as infants.

None of these people are baptized in God's eyes, if as the Bible says, there only one baptism. The long and the short of this story is, if your baptism is not by full immersion, you are not baptized in God's eyes, no matter what your church is telling you.

This book explains why that is the case, and hopefully free you from this mass deception that has beguiled Christians since the 4th century. The question: 'Which baptism' remains one of the utmost importance in Christianity because of what Jesus said in John 3:3-5. He said we cannot go to heaven unless we are born again of water and the Spirit. Acts 2:38 gives us the road map on how one is born again of water and the Spirit.

The most conclusive answer, if the Bible is correct that there is only one baptism, comes straight from the Bible itself. We find it in Acts 8:38-39, that is when the Ethiopian eunuch was baptized. That baptism mirrored the baptism of the Lord Jesus Christ, and I invite you to read it again. "*And he gave orders to stop the chariot. Then both Philip and the eunuch went down into the water and Philip baptized him. When they came out of the water, the Spirit of the Lord suddenly took Philip away, and the eunuch did not see him again, but went on his way rejoicing[13].*"

This is the best example of a Christian baptism in the New Testament.

The teaching leading up to that baptism starts at Acts 8:26. I call this the most conclusive example of a Christian baptism because (1) it happened after Pentecost (2) it was conducted by one of the deacons of the early Church and (3) the Spirit of God was present. It guided the process. God inserted this event in the Bible for a good reason - to guide

---

13 Acts 8:38-39

us. In a sense therefore, the answer to the question 'which baptism' is answered by God himself.

If therefore you have imitated the baptism of the Ethiopian eunuch, which was an exact replica of Jesus' own baptism, you have no doubt received a valid Christian baptism in God's eyes. As I said, the only other time God showed us a baptism in the New Testament was when the Lord Jesus himself was baptized. That was, however, before Pentecost and therefore before the new covenant took effect.

Visually, the two baptisms followed the same script. We should note especially that the baptizer and candidate for baptism went into the water and stood in the water while the ritual was performed. The baptism of Jesus is, however, less representative of all of us than that of the eunuch because Jesus was sinless. The eunuch on the other hand was a sinner, just like you and me.

Secondly, the baptism of Jesus occurred before the Holy Spirit was given his new role as our Helper, our Comforter, the one who came to fill the void left when Jesus ascended to heaven. When we ask people if they have imitated Jesus in baptism, that is what we are talking about – going through the same motions of a baptism as God chose to show us in the Bible.

The primary difference between the baptism of Jesus and that of the eunuch is that in the case of Jesus, it was not for the forgiveness of sins, but to fulfill all righteousness [Matthew 3:15].

Using the eunuch's baptism as our example also avoids the many pitfalls in Christianity today, especially the abuse of Matthew 3:11. That is the verse where John the Baptist tells us that the one coming after him will baptize us with the Holy Spirit and fire. False prophets seize on this verse to claim that in baptism, there are two separate events, a water baptism and baptism by the Holy Spirit and fire. Our counter argument is that in the baptism of the eunuch, we see only one event – someone being dunked into water. We do not see two events.

Unless therefore we are going to argue that the baptism of the eunuch was incomplete, any argument that a Christian baptism comprises two separate events is rendered baseless. In my humble opinion, the two verses [Acts 8:38- 39] provide a complete and conclusive answer to the question: 'Which is the one baptism of the Christian Bible?' The answer is, it is the baptism of the Lord Jesus Christ in the River Jordan; it is the baptism of the Ethiopian eunuch in the desert by Philip, a deacon in the early church.

Acts 1:8, along with Acts 2:38 help us understand the coming of the Holy Spirit even more. Jesus says to his disciples in Acts 1:8, *"… you will receive power when the Holy Spirit comes on you; and you will be my witnesses in Jerusalem, and in all Judea and Samaria, and to the ends of the earth."* That power came to the apostles on Pentecost. So, we cannot pretend the Lord Jesus Christ did not address this issue while he still walked the earth. Acts 2:38 tells us how the same Holy Spirit comes to indwell us, ordinary believers. That is the simplicity of Christianity according to the Bible.

As I pointed out before, Matthew 3:16-17 and Acts 8:38-39 are the only two times in the whole Christian Bible that God **shows us** a Christian baptism. The way it is written is like watching a movie. God shows us a baptism as opposed to telling us about a baptism. The question therefore becomes, if it is so clear in the Bible what a Christian baptism should look like, why are we having this conversation?

The problem of course centers on the Church. While the Bible says there is one God, one Spirit, and one baptism, the Church in practice, disagrees with that. The Church has invented counterfeit baptisms to musk its disobedience of the command by Jesus to baptize believers (Matthew 28:19). As long as the ordinary believer continues to believe they have been baptized when they are given a fake baptism, there is no problem. That, unfortunately, is the world we live in. That is what the Catholic Church and all churches in the Catholic tradition teach and practice. This is despite the reality that there is one baptism according to the Bible, and that reality is not a figment of someone's imagination.

It is in the Bible. It is in Ephesians 4:4-6 and it is partially repeated in 1 Corinthians 12:13. That verse tells us *"For we were all baptized by one Spirit so as to form one body – whether Jews or Gentiles, slave or free – and we were all given the one spirit to drink."*

In Romans 6:3-4 we are offered yet another view of baptism. This time we are told what baptism accomplishes in our Christian lives. The Bible says, *"Or don't you know that all of us who were baptized into Christ Jesus were baptized into his death? We were therefore buried with him through baptism into death in order that, just as Christ was raised from the dead through the glory of the Father, we too may live a new life."* Reference to a new life in this verse means we have been born again of water and the Spirit. Scripture is clear that when we are baptized into Jesus Christ, we are united with him into his death and resurrection. We become new creations in Jesus Christ (2 Corinthians 5:17) and are entitled to all the spiritual blessings that come to us via the cross.

It is only because we observe our churches using more than one baptism that we find ourselves asking the question: 'Which baptism is the 'one' baptism of the Bible?' We are painfully aware that most of our churches baptize by pouring or sprinkling, or by baptizing us as infants, practices that did not exist when Jesus and his apostles walked the earth.

Are these practices valid baptisms in the eyes of God or are they fake baptisms?

Better still, why does the Church so openly contradict the Bible on such a fundamental issue as baptism. Have our churches been blinded by the prince of this world, the devil himself (2 Corinthians 4:4)? The Bible tells us clearly that failure to be properly baptized can disqualify us from entering the kingdom of God. We find that in John 3:3-5? We are also aware that there is no biblical support for these other practices in baptism and there is simply no evidence God has sanctioned them.

So, what is going on?

The Catholics have a built-in excuse for their disobedience of course. For them, the Bible is not their only source of scripture. Yet we also know that if we allow that door to be opened, the Bible will quickly lose its power as the inspired word of God. If on the other hand we subscribe to Sola Scriptura, we should reject the Catholic position and not allow it to enter our Christian lives or remain there?

One of the reasons why Catholic doctrine was able to contaminate Christianity is because there was a time when there was only one church in the world. That church was of course the Catholic Church, the original church of Jesus Christ and his Apostles. For almost 300 years after Jesus' death, that church faced persecution by the devil and his human agents - the Roman Emperors. They ruled the world.

Everything changed, however, when Constantine the Great became Emperor in AD 312. He was a professing Christian on the outside but a sun god worshipper on the inside, a true sheep in wolf 's clothing. Despite claiming to be a Christian, Constantine never got himself baptized during his more than 20-year reign. History records that he was baptized on his deathbed, and that baptism must have been by pouring or sprinkling because one does not get dipped into water when they're lying on their deathbed.

The evidence is that once that church fell under the control of Emperor Constantine in the 4th century, it made some dramatic changes to how one converts to Christianity, and some of those changes were not biblical. The church's evolving doctrine and practice diverged from what Jesus and his apostles taught and practiced to what we know now. It started to develop what it now calls its own doctrine and tradition. At their core these traditions were of the antichrist, in as far as they departed from Christian beliefs and practices of the apostles.

The bishops of this new church did not fear God the way the early church fathers did. For starters, we know they acquiesced when Constantine asked them to disobey God's 4th commandment about resting on the Sabbath. The day of rest (God's Sabbath) was changed from Saturday, the 7th day of the week to Sunday, the 1st day of the week. But the Bible tells us the 7th day of the week is the day God consecrated as the day of rest.

This act of disobedience was just the beginning of the Church's downward spiritual degeneration. Constantine followed this by merging his pagan religious order that worshipped on Sunday into the Church, and the pagans came complete with their own pagan practices and priesthood. These have become part of the so- called Catholic tradition, doctrine, and practice irrespective of whether they offended against God or not. Baptisms that do not conform to the Bible were just the most significant of these practices that offend against God.

For some 13 centuries after Constantine, the church had just about stopped baptizing converts by full immersion completely. They used primarily pouring and sprinkling. The church was finally forced to return to the original baptism of Jesus and the apostles under pressure from the Anabaptists during the Reformation. Even then however, the concession only amounted to paying lip-service to the baptism of the Christian Bible. Paragraph 1239 of the Catechism of the Catholic Church is a clear concession of this fact.

The other act of disobedience by the Church, was its complete disregard of God's 4th commandment that has over the centuries become institutionalized in most Christan countries. Many professing Christians do not realize that our Sunday worship is a man-made rule. Still, many more are unaware that the Roman Catholic Church still has on its books Canon 29 that denies the original Jesus. That Canon says if you continue to obey God on the Sabbath commandment, you are anathema to Jesus.

Now, you tell me, if my Jesus is the same yesterday, today, and forever [Hebrews 13:5], why would I be anathema to him just by obeying him? The possibility therefore remains that the Jesus of the Roman Catholic Church is different from the Jesus of the Apostles. That Jesus never disobeyed his Father in heaven? For those who no longer want to be part of this disobedience against God, the verses that tell us there is one baptism [Ephesians 4:4-6 and 1 Corinthians 12:13] are a great place to start, if you want to be truly born again. False prophets do not factor in their teachings and practices these two verses. For example, I read an article by someone on GotQuestion.org that included the following line: *"Generally speaking, there are two types of baptism: a physical (water) baptism and a spiritual baptism. One is done in water; the other is accomplished in the Holy Spirit."* One wonders where such a statement comes from as it directly contradicts the Bible which tells us there is but one baptism, not two.

To accept this argument would be tantamount to claiming that the baptism of the Ethiopian eunuch [Acts 8:38] was incomplete because we do not see two, but just one baptism, one event. The eunuch was dipped into water and when that process was completed, he was indeed born again, a new creation in Christ Jesus. His baptism was complete, and both Philip and the Spirit of God that had guided the process, disappeared.

Let us also take another look at the baptism of Jesus Christ. *The Bible says "Then Jesus came from Galilee to the Jordan to be baptized by John. But John tried to deter him, saying, "I need to be baptized by you, and do you come to me?" Jesus replied, "Let it be so now; it is proper for us to do this to fulfill all righteousness." Then John consented. As soon as Jesus was baptized,* **he went up** *out of the water. At that moment heaven was opened, and he saw the Spirit of God descending like a dove and alighting on him. And a voice from heaven said, "This is my Son, whom I love; with him I am well pleased[14]."*

We know from scripture therefore that a Christian baptism involves (1) being in water and is done (2) in the presence of the Spirit of God. This could explain the born again of water and the Spirit in John 3:3-5. In both examples of baptism in the New Testament, we know (3) the candidates for baptism and their baptizers both entered the water to perform this sacrament. We also know that (4) water must be plentiful (see John 3:23) to facilitate the process. We know that the candidate for baptism is then (5) dipped into water, which is consistent with the Greek definition of the verb *baptizo* (to baptize) when Jesus still walked the earth.

---

14 Matthew 3:13-17

This therefore must be the baptism Jesus commanded in the Great Commission in Matthew 28:19. We know that to be true because it is the baptism used by the apostles when the eunuch was baptized. This is the baptism that all believers in Jesus Christ should imitate, and as I said before, even the Catholic Church agrees [see paragraph 1239 of its Catechism].

From the baptism of the eunuch, we also have reason to suspect that pouring and sprinkling may not baptize. Why so, you may ask? From Acts 8:26-41 we learn that when Philip and the eunuch came upon some water, the eunuch asked the Apostle whether there was anything that could prevent him from being baptized. The passage is important in this debate because it gives us information that we otherwise would not have. It tells us indirectly that if pouring and/or sprinkling were legitimate methods of baptism, there would have been no reason for Phillip to wait until they came across some water to baptize the eunuch.

Philip could have just sprinkled or poured water from the chariot to baptize the eunuch. We know that the eunuch traveling through the desert must have had water on his chariot. There was therefore more than enough water on board to pour and/or sprinkle to baptize the eunuch. That did not happen because both pouring and sprinkling are post-biblical man-made practices in baptism that were not in play during the ministry of Jesus and his apostles.

Even though this information is not conclusive to disqualify sprinkling and pouring, it helps alert us to the possibility that pouring and sprinkling are suspect as valid baptisms. Neither can therefore be the one baptism of the New Testament.

We also know that nowhere in the Bible are we ever told that Jesus or any of his apostles used pouring, sprinkling, or infant baptisms. At any rate, unless we are now going to say God is a liar, accepting that pouring and/or sprinkling are valid baptisms would be inconsistent with what we learned above that there is only one baptism [Ephesians 4:4-6 & 1 Corinthians 12:13]. We are therefore asking this question 'which baptism' because what we see in our churches seems to be inconsistent with our instruction manual, the Bible.

Secondly, as I stated before, Matthew 3:16-17 and Acts 8:38-39 show us very clearly what God means when he talks about the need for us to be baptized. He also shows us how it is done. Clearly, if there is only one baptism, baptism by full immersion must be the baptism of the Bible. When on Pentecost, the apostle Peter told us to be baptized, there was no vagueness about what was meant. Everyone in Jesus's time knew what was required to be done to be baptized. We know this to be so because the Bible is clear on this point. There is therefore no need for us to go beyond the literal rule to interpret that passage in the Bible.

The apostle Peter on Pentecost in a sense tied all the loose ends of this baptism story together for us by revealing the purpose of a Christian baptism. He said (1) our sins are washed away (forgiven), and (2) the Spirit of God comes to indwell us forever. We also learn from the apostle Paul that at the point of baptism, we become united with Christ into his death and resurrection [Romans 6:3-4]. The apostle Paul did not seek to vary the command by Jesus in the Great Commission or the teaching by the apostle Peter on Pentecost that when we believe, we should be baptized. It was the apostle Peter who also told us when we are baptized, we receive the gift of the Holy Spirit. The apostle Paul was simply explaining how baptism joins us with the Lord Jesus Christ in his death and resurrection. His mission was to explain Jesus, not to redefine him.

Christian charlatans turn this verse into a satanic verse when they argue that baptism is not necessary for salvation. How so, if we need baptism to start to enjoy the saving grace that comes to us via the cross? The verse turns into a satanic verse when it is used to prevent believers from entering the kingdom of God by denying them a baptism that saves.

When we say the counterfeit baptisms of the Church don't baptize, we mean, they do not bring about these same results as baptism by full immersion. They do not wash away our sins, neither do they cause the Holy Spirit to come and indwell us.

They do not unite us with Jesus in his death and resurrection. Without the Holy Spirit indwelling us, we are not 'in Christ', and therefore all the blessings and promises of the New Testament do not flow to us, despite what some of our churches teach.

Remember also that Acts 2:38 is the apostle Peter's answer to a question from the Jews who were gathered and witnessed Pentecost. These people had just witnessed a miracle never before seen. They heard the apostles speaking in tongues, and to their amazement, they understood everything being said in their own language, not in the speaker's language.

This was truly remarkable.

It was a miracle.

While Acts 2:38 in the Bible gives us the guidance we need on how one is born again, the verse itself does not use the words 'born again'. The apostle missed an opportunity to link baptism directly to one being born again. That was unfortunate because the devil eventually found a way to exploit that omission, hence this debate. Christianity was forced to look elsewhere for that link.

We therefore look deeper into what question the Apostle was trying to answer in Acts 2:38. The Jews asked the apostles "Brothers, what shall we do?[15] They were told to repent and be baptized. They were told they will receive the gift of the Holy Spirit when they repent and are baptized. When we look at Mark 16:16, we are told those who believe and are baptized will be saved. So, we know if we follow Acts 2:38 to the letter, we will be saved too. The apostles were putting the command by the Lord Jesus in the Great Commission to baptize all those who believe into action.

The link we are looking for is found in several verses in the Bible but my favorite is 1 Peter 1:3 (ESV) because it is the same apostle Peter

---

15 Acts 2:37

who says *"Blessed be the God and Father of our Lord Jesus Christ, who according to His great mercy has caused us to be born again to a living hope through the resurrection of Jesus Christ from the dead,"*. I use the ESV here to make a point because that version uses born again where the NIV uses 'new birth' instead. The apostle in 1 Peter 1:23 says *"For you have been born again, not of perishable seed, but of imperishable, through the living and enduring word of God." And in 1 Peter 3:20-22, he brings baptism and being saved together when he says "… and this water symbolizes baptism that now saves you also—not the removal of dirt from the body but the pledge of a clear conscience toward God. It saves you by the resurrection of Jesus Christ, who has gone into heaven and is at God's right hand—with angels, authorities and powers in submission to him."*

We can go on and on with this search, but the bottom line is that most theologians believe that Holy Spirit in Acts 2:38 is the 'Spirit and fire' we find in Matthews 3:11. The fact that Jesus did not use the word baptism in John 3:3-5 has become the entry portal through which the devil has been able to enter and introduce counterfeit baptisms into Christianity.

It is estimated that more than half of all Christians, dead and alive, were not baptized by full immersion. They were however made to believe that pouring and sprinkling were valid baptisms in the eyes of God. Recall the Lord Jesus Christ's words that false prophets will prevent you from entering heaven by their false doctrines. Isn't this the very thing we are witnessing here right now? It is the Church that teaches that these baptisms are just as good as the real thing. Some pastors even teach that when one repeats the so-called sinner's prayer, they are born-again, and many professing Christians believe that lie as well. The thinking behind this lie is that when one accepts Jesus as one's Lord and Savior, one is born again.

Having said the above however, we cannot deny that despite the disinformation, the Bible gives us a clear road map to follow to become born-again Christians. It entails one believing in Jesus Christ (John 3:16) and being baptized (Acts 2:38), and as I said, the best verse that brings all this to reality is Mark 16:16, which says *"Whoever believes and is baptized will be saved, but whoever does not believe will be condemned."* False prophets do not like this verse one little bit and have marshaled some arguments about its authenticity. They will tell you it was not in the original text in Mark. But in Acts 2:41 we are told that *"Those who accepted his message were baptized, and about three thousand were added to their number that day."* This confirms the message in Mark 16:16. When you believe in Jesus, you're required to be baptized, which in turn, encores Jesus' message in the Great Commission. The apostles were instructed to make sure we obey everything Jesus had taught them. That is the obedience element in the Great Commission the Church has failed to obey.

And what was that message, you may ask?

It was hearing and believing the good news about Jesus Christ. In Acts 18:8, we are again told the same thing. We are told that *'Crispus, the ruler of the synagogue, believed in the Lord, together with his entire household. And that many of the Corinthians hearing Paul believed and were baptized.'* We are therefore not relying on one Bible verse to state that in Christianity, believing in Jesus Christ and baptism go together and are commanded by the Lord Jesus.

We are also told in the Bible that the Spirit of God will indwell us for the rest of our lives. According to Romans 8:10-11, the Apostle Paul says *"But if Christ is in you, then even though your body is subject to death because of sin, the Spirit gives life because of righteousness. And if the Spirit of him who raised Jesus from the dead is living in you, he who raised Christ from the dead will also give life to your mortal bodies because of his Spirit who lives in you."* This does not preclude the possibility that the Holy Spirit may lie dormant inside you if you go back to your old sinning ways.

Baptism thus equips us with the Spirit of God that never leaves us but can lie dormant inside us if we continue in our old sinning ways.

John 14:16 and Ephesians 1:13-14 are a great help in understanding the permanence of our relationship with Jesus Christ once we accept him as Lord and Savior and are baptized. In John 14:16 Jesus says *"… I will ask the Father, and he will give you another advocate to help you and be with you forever—."* That's further confirmation that once the Holy Spirit comes into us at baptism, he will stay forever.

Ephesians 1:13-14 tells us that we also *"… were included in Christ when you heard the message of truth, the gospel of your salvation. When you believed, you were marked in him with a seal, the promised Holy Spirit, who is a deposit guaranteeing our inheritance until the redemption of those who are God's possession—to the praise of his glory."* We receive this seal, the Holy Spirit when we are baptized, according to Acts 2:38.

Our definition of born-again Christianity is based on this and other teachings by Jesus and his apostles including the teaching from Acts 2:14-41. All these verses in the Bible reinforce the truthfulness of this underlying message. I believe in my heart that Acts 2:38 is the gateway to born-again Christianity. It is difficult to imagine that one who has imitated Jesus in this way would not be born again.

However, the ever-cunning devil always finds a way to exploit our ignorance to his advantage, which only leads to our ruin. In my research on this subject, I came across many articles that agree that the one baptism of the New Testament is baptism by full immersion. Beyond Today (a publication of the Church of God) has a booklet on the subject that I enjoyed reading. While I recommend it, I do not necessarily agree with everything they say. For example, they include in there some verses from Hebrews 6 about the laying of hands as part of the baptism ritual. The laying of hands has nothing whatsoever to do with the baptism of the New Testament. There was no reference to 'laying' of hands when Jesus was baptized in Matthew 3:16-17, and there was none when the Ethiopian eunuch was baptized in Acts 8:38-39.

The idea that laying of hands has something to do with baptism appears to come from Acts 19:6 where the Apostle Paul laid hands on 12 men in Ephesus. What happened here was not meant to redefine the

Christian ritual of baptism, but in a way, amplified some things that may happen to us when we are baptized. The Holy Spirit comes, but we do not see that with our own naked eyes. Yet by faith, we believe that our sins are washed away. Some other gifts may be bestowed, like speaking in tongues and prophesying, etc., but strictly speaking, a Christian baptism is complete the moment you are dipped into the water three times in the name of the Father, of the Son, and of the Holy Spirit. It is the Holy Spirit working in you that then distributes spiritual gifts to the baptized.

The laying of hands is used to bestow a blessing or some other gift or benefit but is not part of the baptism ritual. The best course to follow concerning baptism is to imitate the two baptisms God put in the New Testament as our examples, and by faith, believe that you are now a beneficiary of all the promises of the Bible. The actual teaching in Acts 8 begins at verse 26 and goes all the way to verse 40. There is no mention here of the laying of hands. However, apart from this aside, the Church of God agrees that the one baptism of the Bible is by full immersion.

One cannot force people to believe what they do not want to believe. Those who continue to believe that man-made baptisms like pouring (Catholic Church) and or sprinkling (Lutherans, Anglicans, Presbyterians, and Congregationalists) can transform you into a born-again Christian are clearly misguided. The Methodists, I am told use all three forms of baptism i.e., full immersion, sprinkling, and pouring, which is clearly inconsistent with the 'one' baptism verse in the Bible.

Given the significance of baptism (we cannot enter the kingdom of God without baptism, if born of water and the Spirit means baptism by full immersion), it is therefore disappointing that Christianity has failed so far to settle this issue. The pressure to change this situation should therefore come from congregants like you and me, in churches that use pouring, sprinkling, and infant baptism and hold them out to be genuine baptisms. We need to force them to give us a proper accounting.

They need to answer the ultimate question, which is:- *What will happen to all Christians, dead or alive, who were baptized by pouring, sprinkling or were baptized as infants, if it turns out that God does not accept these man-made practices as genuine?*

The devil has long realized the power of baptism in Christianity. It unites us with the Lord Jesus Christ in his death (the cross) and in his resurrection [Romans 6:3-4]. It is the one thing that gives us a newness in Christ Jesus and confers various blessings on us as believers through His grace. These promises are only available to those who have gone through the ritual of baptism, and the devil does not like that.

The biggest benefit of baptism is of course the promise that our past sins are forgiven and that our new sins are forgiven when we confess them and ask God for forgiveness. That means, going forward, we are the 'untouchables' of God because all we need to do is confess our present mistakes to God, and ask Him to forgive us for those mistakes, and it's done. The Bible says it in this way: *"If we confess our sins, he is faithful and just and will forgive us our sins and purify us from all unrighteousness[16]."* Christians who pray every day accomplish this by simply including in their prayers a request for forgiveness. Others recite the Lord's prayer that includes the line *"forgive us our debts as we also forgive our debtors.[17]"*

As I pointed out before however, there is a caution to this promise of God's forgiveness and we find it in Hebrews 10:27 where we are told that *"If we deliberately keep on sinning [continue to sin] after we have received the knowledge of the truth, no sacrifice for sins is left, but only a fearful expectation of judgment and of raging fire that will consume the enemies of God."* This passage in the Bible serves as a reminder that there is a limit to God's grace of forgiveness if we continue to sin after we are baptized, which is true of most of us. How this verse operates in real life is difficult to assess since at one extreme God tells us once we are 'in Christ', we are punished ultimately only for unconfessed sin and the sin

---

16 John 1:9
17 Matthew 6:12

of blasphemy. That means if we get into the habit of confessing our sins every day, we should be covered.

Other verses that loom large in this debate include 1 John 1:7 which says, *"But if we walk in the light, as he is in the light, we have fellowship with one another, and the blood of Jesus, his Son, purifies us from all sin."* For me, this is huge. I like this verse because it also covers believers who might die unexpectedly as in an accident. They don't have a chance for that last-minute confession before they die, but they are saved because they have walked in the light since their baptism.

With baptism therefore, the devil was totally defeated at the cross. This was a 'get- out-of-jail-free' card handed to Christians on a platter. The devil had to find a way somehow to erase this advantage. For almost 300 years, the devil tried persecuting and excommunicating Christian leaders using his human agents, but to no avail. That was until he found Constantine the Great. One of the most effective tools the devil has used against Jesus was getting the Church, once under Constantine, to believe it was now okay to disobey God.

The first act of disobedience was switching God's Sabbath from Saturday, the 7th day of the week to Sunday, the 1st day of the week. Once the Church agreed to disobey God, the devil had gained a foothold into Christianity. He immediately introduced pagan practices into the Church, including baptism by pouring and sprinkling. The Church literally abandoned baptism by full immersion. We can see the result for ourselves. The devil used the very church Jesus founded to redefine baptism by introducing counterfeit baptisms into the Church based on the teaching of the Didache, a document that is not part of the inspired word of God.

CHAPTER 4

ARE YOU SAVED

*Whoever **believes** and is baptized will be **saved**, but whoever does not believe will be condemned.*

Mark 16:16

Peter replied, "Repent and be baptized, every one of you, in the name of Jesus Christ for the forgiveness of your sins. And you will receive the gift of the Holy Spirit.

Acts 2:38

One of the biggest misconceptions about being born again is a false equivalency people put between being 'born again' and being 'saved'. The Bible uses the word saved to mean different things in the progression from first hearing the good news about Jesus to your baptism, depending on the context. The word saved is used for what happens before baptism as well as what happens during baptism and what happens after baptism. The saved that matters is the one that allows you to receive the gift of the Holy Spirit, and that happens only when you're in the process of being baptized.

Typically, you are standing in water with the baptizer also in water, and you are dunked in water three times in the name of the Father, of the son, and of the Holy Spirit. When that process ends and you come out of water, your conversion is complete [Acts 8:38-39]. The Bible says we are saved the moment we believe, but we are still not saved, if that makes sense to you at all. Therefore, seizing on every verse that says you are saved, or you will be saved, or you're being saved does not help us understand who is saved and who is not saved.

Context is important.

For instance, we are told that those who believe in Jesus will be saved (Romans 10:9-10), but these people are already baptized believers in Jesus Christ. We find a similar statement in Acts 16:31 concerning the jailer and his household, but in this case, baptism had not yet taken place. In John 3:16 we are told God sent his only begotten son so whoever believed in him would not perish. One assumes that in this verse, not perish means they will be saved. But in Mark 16:16, the Bible goes further and tells us those who believe and are baptized will be saved.

So, which is which?

Simply quoting these verses without context can be misleading. One is saved the moment they hear the good news about Christ and believe (John 3:16) but something more is required to seal your believing in Jesus Christ (Mark 16:16 & Ephesians 1:13), and that one thing, is baptism. Until that happens however, you might be saved in that sense but you're not yet 'born again' (John 3:3-5 & 2 Corinthians 5:17). All these verses work together. God seals us with his Holy Spirit when we are baptized (Acts 2:38 and Ephesians 1:13-14).

The best way to conceptualize this is to think of a conveyor belt. The moment you hear the good news about Jesus, and you believe, you hop on this conveyor belt, and you are saved. You're however not yet born again. The destination of this conveyor belt is the baptismal River, pool, lake or ocean where your baptism will take place. It is only then that you have reached the saved in the Great Commission, the saved in Mark 16:16.

Yes, you were saved the moment you hopped onto this imaginary conveyor belt, but your being saved is a process that ends in your being dumped into this collection of water where you will be baptized. You control the speed of this conveyor belt. You can fast track it and get to the lake the same day or take your time and get there when you are ready. It's all up to you, but as long as you are on this conveyor belt, you are saved because you have found Jesus.

The Church has managed to convince many that the moment you get on that conveyer belt you're saved. The reality is you have started your journey to be saved, and you're now in the process of being saved. If you happen to die in that state, you're not born again, and will not enter the kingdom of God according to Jesus in John 3:3-5. Hope this graphic helps somebody.

To recap: The Bible tells us we need to be born again of water and the Spirit to enter the kingdom of God [John 3:3-5]. In Mark 16:16, the Bible tells us if we believe and are baptized, we will be saved. In this verse therefore "saved" means you're born again because you have received the baptism commanded by the Lord Jesus in the Great Commission [Matthew 28:19-20], and you now have the Holy Spirit living in you according to Acts 2:38 that provides us with the road map.

Yet the Bible tells us elsewhere that those who endure to the end will be saved (Matthew 24:13). One can see clearly how the Bible uses the same word to mean different things, depending on the context. That means if the goal of your Christianity is to go to heaven, then you need to be born again [John 3:3-5]. But the same Bible tells us we need to endure to the end to make that a reality (Matthew 24:13). That means, if you backslide along the way, that might not happen for you. We find this guidance in Hebrews 10:27 which says if we continue to sin after we have come to know the truth about Jesus, the saving power in the blood of Jesus will no longer be available to us. The many references to one being saved we see in the Bible do not always mean you're born again.

Now, there is something else that might help you figure this out more easily. The saved we find in Romans 10:9-10 and Ephesians 2:4-10 is not talking about a pre- baptized you but a post-baptized you. The apostle Paul is talking to people who are already saved because they have been united with Jesus Christ through baptism. Most of the epistles we read in the New Testament are to converts, members of the church. That means they have complied with the instructions in Acts 2:38 and already have the Holy Spirit indwelling them. Failure to recognize this distinction has allowed the devil to wreak havoc on the Christian community for centuries.

In this connection, please read the passage below from Ephesians 2, in full for context, starting with verse 4. That passage says *"But because of his great love for us, God, who is rich in mercy, made us alive with Christ even when we were dead in transgressions—it is by grace you have been saved. And God raised us up with Christ and seated us with him in the heavenly realms in Christ Jesus, in order that in the coming ages he might show the incomparable riches of his grace, expressed in his kindness to us in Christ Jesus. For it is by grace you have been saved, through faith—and this is not from yourselves, it is the gift of God— not by works, so that no one can boast. For we are God's handiwork, created in Christ Jesus to do good works, which God prepared in advance for us to do."*

We are talking about a born-again Christian here, a person who is already united with Christ through baptism. Reference to God raised us up with Christ are to his resurrection as in Romans 6:3-4. False prophets will omit the last verse [verse 10] for a good reason. That verse ties everything back to Jesus Christ and his sacrifice on the cross. They will not highlight that because it defeats their purpose of misleading you into believing that one is born again merely by believing in Jesus Christ. They will not tell you that to partake in the spiritual benefits that f low from the cross, including the saving grace this passage references here, you need to receive a proper baptism.

Romans 6:3-4 conveys the idea here more directly when it says *"Or don't you know that all of us who were baptized into Christ Jesus were baptized into his death? We were therefore buried with him through baptism into death in order that, just as Christ was raised from the dead through the glory of the Father, we too may live a new life."*

Lawyers will grasp the underlying concept here more easily than the rest of us. In contract law, they use the concept of 'offer and acceptance' to underscore the idea that there is no contract between you and a seller of goods and services until you accept his offer. You accept the offer by buying the goods and/or services being offered.

A merchant who displays his/her wares in the marketplace is merely making you an offer. There is no contract between you and the merchant until you accept the offer by buying the item offered. That is exactly what God did when He offered his Son on the cross as a sacrifice for our sins. There is no contract between you and God until you accept his offer of freedom from sin by believing in Jesus [faith in Jesus] and getting baptized. That's when you get the Holy Spirit, at which point, you're really born again.

Mark 16:16 tells us we need to be baptized to be saved. Acts 1:4-5 and Acts 2:38 tells us when we are baptized, we get the gift of the Holy Spirit and Acts 1:4-5 tells us about the Holy Spirit. That passage says *"On one occasion, while he was eating with them, he gave them this command: "do not leave Jerusalem, but wait for the gift my father promised, which you have heard me speak about. For john baptized with water, but in a few days you will be baptized with the holy spirit."*

The reference here is to the promise by Jesus in John 14:26 to send the apostles an advocate, who will help them remember everything Jesus had taught them. That advocate was the Holy Spirit. The rest of us receive that same Holy Spirit when we are baptized. For the apostles, their transformation came in two steps. They were baptized before the Holy Spirit took over from Jesus. Pentecost was the day the process was completed for them. It was clearly a two-event process for them. For the rest of us however, baptism became a one-event process according to Acts 2:38. It tells that those who obey and are baptized receive the promised Holy Spirit upon being baptized.

Acts 2:38 in this sense completes the narrative we first encountered in Acts 1:4-5 that tells us *"Exalted to the right hand of god, he has received from the Father the promised Holy Spirit and has poured out what you now see and hear."*

The devil knows all this better than you and your pastor. That is why he, the devil, introduced counterfeit baptisms into Christianity to deny you the freedom you deserve when you're baptized by full immersion. The idea that you get the Holy Spirit merely by accepting Jesus as your Lord and Savior is part of the deception. Accepting Jesus as your Lord and Savior entails believing in Jesus Christ and being baptized.

When we do that, we receive the gift of the Holy Spirit according to Acts 2:38. That means receiving the Holy Spirit in this sense is a by-product of your baptism.

This is the basic teaching of Acts 2:38.

But many Christian denominations disregard Acts 2:38 and have developed their own man-made theories about baptism and being born again based on misapplying Bible verses. In my other book "CHRISTIAN SATANIC VERSES", I explain why I call all verses that have been abused or corrupted 'satanic verses'. These are verses God meant to mean one thing but the false prophet has misinterpreted to mean something else. Some of the apostle Paul's writings in the New Testament are misinterpreted in this way to mislead. They are used in this way serve the devil's interest of opposing God.

Let's look at one of the most confusing (to me) of these abused verses and how it has been abused. In Romans 10:9-11, the apostle Paul teaches that *"If you declare with your mouth, "Jesus is Lord," and believe in your heart that God raised him from the dead, you will be saved. For it is with your heart that you believe and are justified, and it is with your mouth that you profess your faith and are saved.*

The 'save' here can be confusing, at least to me. It seems to belong to someone who is still on that conveyor belt as in John 3:16, and the apostle seems to be quoting John 3:16, i.e., *"Anyone who believes in him will never be put to shame."* Those who have heard the good news about

Jesus, and have believed but lack the required baptism to seal this deal with God are still not saved as in born again.

The apostle then says, 'it is with your heart that you believe and are justified'. But when he defines justified in Galatians 2:15-16, he says *"We who are Jews by birth and not sinful Gentiles know that a person is not justified by the works of the law, but by faith in Jesus Christ. So we, too, have put our faith in Christ Jesus that we may be justified by faith in Christ and not by the works of the law, because by the works of the law no one will be justified."* This tells us the justified here has something to do with Jesus Christ, something that can only come to us after baptism.

I was still confused however, so I took my research to Barnes Bible Commentary, but the explanation there still did not resolve my issue. I also tried Matthew Henry and though the explanation there was better, I came out of this with the following thought: - the apostle's audience were Jews who had rejected Jesus; the apostle was using John 3:16 to explain that those who reject Jesus will be condemned but that once we accept Jesus as our Lord and Savior, we are saved (remember analogy of the conveyor belt, and verse 10 where believing and justification are brought together. My issue here, or rather, the source of my confusion, is still what exactly did the apostle mean.

The Dictionary says justification in the theological sense is a process by which God declares us innocent or guiltless in His eyes. The Oxford Languages says justification is "the action of declaring or making [one] righteous in the sight of God."

Now, here is the problem with this abuse of these verses by false prophets in the context of Acts 2:38, they focus on the words believe in Jesus Christ and forget that after you believe in Jesus, you're required to take some action, and that action is getting baptized (Mark 16:16). This is shown most clearly in the baptism of the jailer and his household in Acts 16:29-33. When he asks the apostles what he should do to be saved, he is told to believe in Jesus, and only after believing is he then baptized. That should tell us that without baptism, we're not there yet. You have heard the good news about Jesus, and you have believed, but you have yet to be baptized for the forgiveness of your sins. It is during that process of baptism that one receives the Holy Spirit.

What confuses me is that people seem to equate believing in Jesus as one and the same thing as faith in Jesus. This is not correct. The apostle James explains this best (James 2:19) when he says "You believe that there is one God. Good! Even the demons believe that – and shudder." When the apostle says this, he does not mean that demons have faith, but that demons know there is one God because they know the truth, they were once in heaven with God, but they are now fallen angels. Knowing the truth requires no faith.

We can reinforce our knowledge of faith here by going back to the biblical definition of faith in Hebrews 11:1 – "Now faith is the assurance of things hoped for, the conviction of things not seen." You might also read the Amplified translation of the same verse for reinforcement. To have faith in Jesus therefore means that after you believed, you went ahead and obeyed Jesus's command to be baptized (Matthew 28:19 and Mark 16:16).

You can see clearly how complicated verses like those that use believing in Jesus Christ and faith in Jesus Christ can be difficult to understood, and therefore lend themselves open to abuse. That is why Mark 16:16 remains a better guide on this subject. That is the scripture that says those who believe and are baptized will be saved. You're clearly not saved in this sense if you have not yet been baptized.

Acts 22:16 is another helpful verse. Here Ananias says to Saul before he becomes Paul, *"And now what are you waiting for? Get up, be baptized and wash your sins away, calling on his name."* This confirms that believing in Jesus is just the beginning of your journey in Christ. You have embarked on the road that leads you to becoming a born- again Christian, but you're not there yet until you're baptized.

Incidentally, the Bible tends to talk about the same event from one or more perspectives. The narrative of Paul's encounter with Jesus on the road to Damascus is a good example of this. There are two versions of this event in the Bible. I quoted the first above, and the second is as narrated by Paul himself in Acts 9:1-19. The first omits many details of the event that are in the second version, but the two accounts do not contradict each other. People should always bear that in mind about the Bible. False prophets, including many of our established churches have developed practices that contradict scripture, especially with respect to baptism and the Great Commission.

Before you argue with me about baptism, ask yourself if your practices are compliant with Jesus's command to baptize. Don't try and hoodwink us by inventing fake baptisms so you can hide behind them to claim compliance. You can fool mortals most of the time, but you cannot fool God.

In the Great Commission, Jesus commands his apostles [the Church] to go and make disciples of all nations, baptizing them in the name of the Father, of the Son, and of the Holy Spirit, and teaching them everything he had commanded them. The churches are not compliant. They musk their noncompliance by using fake baptisms. Others make phony arguments such those of the "grace alone/faith alone" brigade.

Once you have digested the message of these passages in the Bible, go back and review Acts 2:38 again and see how it is a practical implementation of the command by Jesus Christ in The Great Commission. If you start reading Acts 2 from verse 14, you also see that this teaching mirrors the part that says, 'when you hear the good news about Jesus, you should repent and be baptized'.

Who should we blame for the wholesale disobedience of Jesus' command in the Great Commission to baptize? The Church of course. It is the Church that dropped the ball. I have devoted Chapter 9 to a discussion about the role of the Church in all this confusion.

John 3:16 also offers us some more insights into this question.

That verse says, *"For God so loved the world that he gave his one and only Son, that whoever believes in him shall not perish but have eternal life."* Taken in isolation, it means all you need to do is believe in Jesus

Christ and you will have eternal life. The real question therefore is what does it mean to believe in Jesus Christ? It is not just an abstract term but entails some prescribed actions to activate your believing in Jesus Christ. In this regard, Mark 16:16 moves us forward by telling us *"Whoever believes and is baptized will be saved, but whoever does not believe will be condemned."* Here, we are told believing alone is not enough. You should believe and be baptized, which ties in with the apostle Peter's teaching on Pentecost that we should be baptized for the forgiveness of sins.

Pastors like Joel Osteen are often criticized for teaching that if one repeats the so- called sinner's prayer, which as we have seen above comes from Romans 10:9-10, one is born again. This is clearly false teaching because it gives you a false sense of security to believe that you're already born again when that is not the case. This criticism would vanish if Joel Osteen simply substituted 'saved' for 'born again' in his sermons.

Another important thing to consider in this connection is that the teachings of the apostle Paul came more than 25 years after Pentecost. What he said in his writings was never meant to contradict or revise Acts 2:38. Indeed, the apostle himself followed Acts 2:38, and baptized believers by full immersion. We see this same instruction first given in the Great Commission (Matthew 28:19-20) and Mark 16:16 repeated in Acts 2:38, 1 Peter 3:21, Romans 6:3, John 1:33, Acts 22:16, 1 Corinthians 6:11, and several other verses. These apostles were spreading the gospel and baptizing and Paul, as Saul, was persecuting them. He was present when Steven was martyred. This time element needs to be factored into his later contributions to scripture.

One can see clearly how some churches have turned the above verses into 'satanic verses' by simply misinterpreting them in a manner that misleads many professing Christians and lead them away from salvation. They are satanic because in their hands, they serve the interests of the devil rather than those of our Creator. Once corrupted, these verses are then used to deny us that one thing that clothes us with Jesus Christ, and that is, a proper baptism.

While the apostle who wrote them says clearly in Romans 6:3-4, 'we are united with Jesus through baptism', these churches by-pass that by using fake baptisms to deceive believers into thinking they have been baptized as called for in the Great Commission. This is the deception we should fight to reverse. As I pointed out above, the abused verses are used to contradict Jesus' command in the Great Commission [Matthew 28:19-20] that we should be baptized.

Another verse that has been turned into a satanic verse is Ephesians 2:8-10 which says *"For it is by grace you have been saved, through faith— and this is not from yourselves, it is the gift of God— not by works, so that no one can boast. For we are God's handiwork, created in Christ Jesus to do good works, which God prepared in advance for us to do."* How can you be 'created in Christ' if you have not been united with him through baptism [Romans 6:3-4]? False prophets deliberately drop verse 10 in their sermons. They will just refer to verses 8 and 9 and omit verse 10 because it ties them back to the Lord Jesus Christ. That omission is deliberate. It is done to mislead you. Without verse 10, the teaching becomes 'baptism is not necessary because *we are saved by grace alone through faith [in Jesus].* Faith in Jesus Christ entails obeying his commands, and one of those commands is in the Great Commission, and it is that you should be baptized for the forgiveness of sins, so you can [now] receive the Holy Spirit.

The grace in this scripture comes to us through Jesus Christ's sacrifice on the cross. We call this 'saving grace'. The same apostle Paul whose writings they misquote and misapply is the same apostle who told us in Romans 6:4-7 *"We were therefore*

buried with him (Jesus Christ) through baptism into death in order that, just as Christ was raised from the dead through the glory of the Father, we too may live a new life. For if we have been united with him in a death like his, we will certainly also be united with him in a resurrection like his. For we know that our old self was crucified with him so that the body ruled by sin might be done away with that we should no longer be slaves to sin— because anyone who has died has been set free from sin."

As usual, false prophets will not quote the whole passage but only the part that serves their purpose of supporting their false narrative about baptism. Here, the apostle makes it clear this grace belongs to people who have been united with Christ through baptism [Romans 6:3-4]. Anyone who has yet to be baptized is not included in this verse, and therefore does not have this grace. Yet the false prophets use this circular reasoning to mislead people not yet in Christ into believing they're already in Christ and therefore are entitled to all the spiritual benefits of Christian hood.

I have devoted the next chapter to a discussion of grace. It explains what grace brings to believers when they are properly baptized. In this connection, we should study 1 Corinthians 6:11 closely. It tells us that 'we were washed (redeemed), we were sanctified, we were justified in the name of the Lord Jesus Christ, and in the Spirit of our God.'

In summary, let us return to the teaching by the apostle Peter on the day of Pentecost. He said, if we hear the good news about Jesus and believe, we ought to do certain things, and what are those certain things? We need to repent and be baptized for the forgiveness of sins. When we look at the baptism of the Ethiopian eunuch, repenting seems to occur when we submit ourselves to baptism for the forgiveness of sins. Our 'old' selves remain in the water and only our newness of life awaits us. We do not see the eunuch listing his sins before he is baptized. Submitting to baptism therefore seems to take care of the need to list all our past sins in this new dispensation with Jesus Christ.

Every Christian must decide for themselves however whether sprinkling and pouring will bring about the same spiritual results as baptism by full immersion. Will your sins be washed away when water is poured or sprinkled on you in this church inspired baptism? Will the Spirit of God come and indwell you during this man-made baptism? My simple answer is that the Bible does not teach that. You only believe that because your church has told you that.

Always keep in mind the reality that all this false teaching can be removed from your life when you take one small step that takes less than 5 minutes to accomplish – that is, getting yourself baptized by full immersion.

It might be useful for you as an individual to take a few minutes of your time and list for yourself the reason(s) why you have not been baptized by full immersion this far. Why have you not imitated Jesus in baptism child of God, even as you have devoted your life to God and your church? Why haven't you complied with Matthew 28:19, Mark 16:16 and Acts 2:38?

CHAPTER 5

GRACE

"But God demonstrates his own love for us in this: While we were still sinners, Christ died for us."

Romans 5:8

The Church preaches correctly that we receive grace from God, which is true, but when you know the truth, you need also to ask these two questions:

- What exactly is grace?

- Which grace are we talking about?

I will try and answer both questions in this chapter.

I believe there are two types of grace in the Bible, and I will call the first type of grace 'universal' grace, and the second type of grace, 'Christian grace' or 'in Christ grace'. We find this Christian grace in the New Testament.

God's universal grace is available to all His creations irrespective of where in the world they call home or their belief system. We find God's universal grace in the last sentence in this passage from Matthews 5:43-45 which says *"You have heard that it was said, 'Love your neighbor and hate your enemy. But I tell you, love your enemies and pray for those who persecute you, that you may be children of your Father in heaven. He causes his sun to rise on the evil and the good, and sends rain on the righteous and the unrighteous.* "The passage mentions His rain and sun, but we can add many others to that list including the air we breathe, the food we eat, and the like. This grace is available to everyone – Jew and Gentile alike. You can go to China, Japan, India, Africa, Europe or the Americas, and you will find this grace there, and in abundance.

This has led Christians to define grace as a free unmerited gift of favor and love God gives to all. The underlying idea is that it is free, it is unmerited, it is available to all, it is undeserved and is ref lective of God's benevolent character.

Now, let's look at grace from a slightly different angle. We can say God's grace gave us food to eat. In Genesis 1:29-30 we are told, *"Then God said, "I give you every seed- bearing plant on the face of the whole earth and every tree that has fruit with seed in it. They will be yours for food. And to all the beasts of the earth and all the birds in the sky and all the creatures that move along the ground—everything that has the breath of life in it—I give every green plant for food." And it was so."*

God later added meat to our diet when he blessed Noah and his sons in Genesis 9:3 where He said *"Everything that lives and moves about will be food for you. Just as I gave you the green plants, I now give you everything."*

Again, this is God's grace that is available to everyone, but this is not entirely free as in the first case of the sun and the rain, is it? We now must do something before we can put that food on the table. At a minimum, we must make some physical effort to go gather this food [fruits, vegetables, meat, fish, etc.] before we can eat it. If we need some rice, wheat, maize, potatoes with our meat and vegetables, we must cultivate or go hunting or fishing to get it to our tables.

This grace is still free because God made sure his creations have access to something to eat. However, food does not fall like manna from heaven. We must do something before we can eat it. Even in the case of manna from heaven, the Jews had to go out and gather the manna to eat. If you did not do that, you starved to death. We however see the grace in these last two verses as free because like a mother of a newborn, God anticipated our need for sustenance and provided for it.

The free gifts from God in the New Testament, as opposed to the Old Testament, are however conditional. In John 1:16-17, the Bible says, *"Out of his fullness we have all received grace in place of grace already given. For the law was given through Moses; grace and truth came through Jesus Christ.* This passage in the Bible gives us a clue that apart from the universal grace that was there before, there is additional grace that has come to us through Jesus.

Who gets this grace?

Unfortunately, the Church does not teach this because it would undermine the deception that first entered Christianity when Constantine the Great started his reign in 312 AD. As a result of this deception, we do not focus too much on the difference between universal grace and grace that comes to us via the cross.

Is this new grace available to everyone?

A key verse to understanding conditional grace that comes to us via the cross is Romans 6:3-4 that we have already discussed. The verse tells us that those of us who are in Christ have been united with the Lord Jesus Christ through baptism. It follows then that unless we have been united with Jesus [Romans 6:3-6] through the one baptism of the Bible [Ephesians 4:4-6], we cannot partake in this grace even though the Church teaches otherwise.

Romans 8:9 can be helpful here as well, because it tells us we cannot be in Christ if the Spirit of God is not in us. Fair enough, how do we get the Spirit of God into us?

Acts 2:38 tells us we get that Spirit of God during baptism. That means, biblically, it is a false claim to say the Holy Spirit indwells you when you have not been baptized. To musk the deception that you have not been baptized and therefore do not have the Holy Spirit indwelling you, the Church uses fake baptisms. Therefore, even though you never received the one baptism of the Bible, the Church has managed to convince many the fake baptisms of pouring, sprinkling and infant baptism also baptize. It has falsely held them out to be the real thing. That is the heart of the deception we are talking about here.

While all Christians are taught by the Church that they have received Christian grace, this is not true if one has not been united with Jesus Christ through baptism, and that baptism is by full immersion. We can now formulate a challenge question based on this understanding that if you have not been baptized by full immersion, i.e., you were given a man-made baptism of pouring, sprinkling, and or infant baptism, you're not entitled to all the promises of God in the New Testament. These blessings and promises are conditioned on you being baptized. A good example of this is Philippians 4:19 that says God will meet all our needs according to the riches of his glory in Christ Jesus.

Let your church or your pastor, your small Bible Study group, seminary study group or you individually come forward and refute this statement as part of the $30,000 Book Challenge. In this respect, Romans 3:20-24 will aid you in your research. That passage in the Bible says *"Therefore by the deeds of the law there shall no flesh be justified in his sight: for by the law is the knowledge of sin. But now the righteousness of God without the law is manifested, being witnessed by the law and the prophets; Even the righteousness of God which is by faith of Jesus Christ unto all and upon all them that believe: for there is no difference: For all have sinned, and come short of the glory of God; Being justified freely by his grace through the redemption that is in Christ Jesus:"*

That means we are redeemed by the power in the blood of Jesus. Note the use of two words in this passage that are defined in terms of faith in Jesus Christ, and those words are (1) justified and (2) redemption. According to the Bible, we are redeemed by the blood of Jesus[18], and we are justified by the blood of Jesus[19]. How does the blood of Jesus come to work for you if you have not yet been united with him through baptism?

---

[18] 1Peter 1:18-19; Rev 12:11
[19] Romans 5:9

In all honesty, we cannot describe the grace that comes to us via the cross as undeserved or as free in the same way God gives us the sun and the rain. The Bible tells us it is conditional. We must do something to receive it. Unless you're in Christ, this 'in Christ' grace is not available to you.

False prophets have many deceptive arguments to counter this truth, and the strongest is that of works in the Bible. Ephesians 2:8-10 is their vehicle for this deception. This is a good example of how a Bible verse is easily turned into a satanic verse. That passage in the Bible says, *"For it is by grace you have been saved, through faith—and this is not from yourselves, it is the gift of God— not by works, so that no one can boast. For we are God's handiwork, created in Christ Jesus to do goof works, which God prepared in advance for us to do."* The passage encourages believers to unite with Jesus through baptism so they can enjoy the grace that came to us through the cross. False prophets turn this same passage into a satanic verse by dropping that last sentence that references Christ Jesus (verse 10). They will argue that getting baptized is 'works' around and use the same verse to discourage believers from being baptized. All that because they misunderstand the works referenced here.

The Bible encourages believers to do good works. In James 2:14-17 we are told *"What good is it, my brothers and sisters, if someone claims to have faith but has no deeds? Can such faith save them? Suppose a brother or a sister is without clothes and daily food. If one of you says to them, "Go in peace; keep warm and well fed," but does nothing about their physical needs, what good is it? In the same way, faith by itself, if it is not accompanied by action, is dead."* Good works are the essence of Christianity, as this passage says. What the apostle Paul was saying is, it is not by works that we are saved. Therefore, people should not expect their good works to save them, as in going to heaven if they are not in compliance with Jesus' command in the Great Commission to baptize all who believe. He is in effect saying that's not how this works. You need to have faith in Jesus so that by grace, you will be saved. To have that grace, you need to be in Christ, and the only way to be clothed with Christ is through baptism. To hear the false prophet speak, a simple act of obedience (command in Matthew 28:19) to get baptized is now classified as works. But in that same verse Jesus commands this obedience. God commanded the apostles (the Church) to teach us to obey. The verse is turned into a satanic verse when it encourages believers to do the exact opposite of what God intended – obedience. It is then used to argue that requiring believers to be baptized is requiring them to be saved by works. That's not what the Bible is teaching here.

With universal grace like the sun and the rain on the other hand, we do not have to do anything to receive it. Just as the church falsely teaches that we are saved without biblical baptism, it also teaches that we get grace that comes via the cross without a proper baptism. Some even teach that we get 'in Christ' grace without baptism. They then go on to argue that it is this same grace, grace that you do not have in the first place, that now mysteriously saves you. Others even go further to argue that this grace, that the Church has falsely attributed to you, is all you need to be saved. The "grace alone through faith alone brigade" is especially vocal here.

Understanding this truth will help you understand part of the deception that is behind today's Christianity. In the case of this Christian grace for example, we must not only believe in Jesus Christ, but we must have also received the one baptism of the New Testament [Ephesians 4:4-6] to receive it [Mark 16:16].

As I said, this is not works but a simple act of obedience. It is required. Note that Mark 16:16 does not tell us what happens to people who believe but are not baptized, which happens to be the group where most modern-day Christians must belong. So, what happens to them.

The best answer to that question is "nothing". This is so primarily because they have hopped on that imaginary conveyor belt that leads to baptism but have yet to reach the required destination. If they die in that state, John 3:3-5 provides us with the answer, and that answer is that they will not enter the kingdom of God; heaven, to you and me.

Incidentally, I read a great article by Dr. Ray Pritchard on this subject titled "What is Baptism? Its Meaning and Importance in Christianity[20]". It offers some interesting insights into the question of what happens to believers who are not baptized. I suppose the best answer is the one I've just given above, nothing.

They are not condemned, primarily because they have hopped on that imaginary conveyor belt to salvation. If they never make it to that baptismal pool (ocean, lake, river, pool, whatever), the Bible tells us clearly what they lack, and here below is my partial list:

They are not new creations in Jesus Christ (2 Corinthians 5:17),

they are not reborn spiritually (2 Corinthians 5:17);

they are not born again (John 3:3-5);

they will not enter the kingdom of God (John 3:3);

they are not united with Christ in his death and resurrection (Romans 6:3-4);

they are not saved (Mark 16:16)

[21]they do not have the Holy Spirit in them (Acts 2:38);

their sins have not been forgiven (Acts 2:38),

they do not have what I call Christian grace, etc.

So, while Mark 16:16 does not tell us what happens to believers who are not baptized, scripture does. Christian grace is not available to everyone. The Jews don't have it. The Moslems don't have it, and professing Christians, being people who believe in Christ but have not been baptized by full immersion do not have it. They believe, according to Mark 16:16, but they have yet to obey the Mster's command to obey. They have refused to obey Jesus' command to be baptized. They are not saved in the sense of being born again.

---

[20] Ray Pritchard, What is Baptism? www.christianity.com/wiki/christian-terms May 28, 2024
[21]

The Church will not discuss Christian grace in these terms because that would expose the lie behind its teaching about grace. They want all Christians, baptized or not; to believe they have received this grace. This is understandable. The Church does not want to disenfranchise millions of professing Christians from believing they have been baptized and therefore have this Christian grace. Your pastor will give a sermon on Philippians 4:19 that says *"my God will meet all my needs according to the riches of his glory in Christ Jesus"* for example, but that is not entirely true without this one baptism of the Bible, is it?

So, who is entitled to this promise?

All Christians who have been baptized into Christ Jesus are entitled to this promise. Those who have been fake baptized by pouring, sprinkling and infant baptisms however are not entitled to this promise, unless God accepts these man- made baptisms as valid. My last reading of the Bible suggests that God does not approve of man-made rules that override his commands. God says, "They worship me in vain; their teachings are merely human rules[22]."

My question to you child of God is if you believe there is a heaven and hell, why are you taking a chance of not going to heaven by resisting the one baptism of the Bible? Who has blinded you to that truth? The Christian community, unlike the Jewish and Moslems communities, therefore, needs to rethink their Christianity on this basis.

Let me now discuss several of these blessings that come to us by way of the cross.

According to the apostle Paul, they are conditional on us being united with Jesus Christ [Romans 6:3-6] in his death and resurrection through the one baptism of the Bible, [Ephesians 4:4-6]. We therefore need to be compliant to receive this grace.

<u>Gift of the Holy Spirit</u>

We find this grace in Acts 2:38 and it only comes when we are baptized by full immersion. There is no biblical evidence that man-made baptisms

---

[22] Matthew 15:9

of the Church bring about this gift, even though the Church preaches otherwise.

Forgiveness of Sin

Baptism since John the Baptist has always been for the forgiveness of sins [Mark 1:4; Matthew 3:11]. We also find this grace in 1 John 1:9 where we are told "If we confess our sins, he is faithful and just and will forgive us our sins and purify us fro*m all unrighteousness." This is all about Jesus. 1 John 1:7 is clear that "… if we walk in the light, as he is in the light, we have fellowship with one another, and the blood of Jesus, his Son, purifies us from all[b] sin."* The Bible is clear that one must be in Christ Jesus to enjoy this grace. It is the blood of Jesus that makes all this possible. Our challenge question on this subject is how does the blood of Jesus work for you if you have not been united with him through baptism [Romans 6:3-6]?

Redemption

Redemption in the Bible means deliverance from sin and freedom from captivity through the atonement of the death of Jesus Christ. Romans 3:23 says, *"Christ's redemption has freed us from guilt, being justified freely by His grace through the redemption that is in Christ."* In Christ in this passage means you have been united with him through baptism. Galatians 3:13 tells us that *"Christ redeemed us frum the curse of the law by becoming a curse for us -for it is written, "Cursed is everyone who is hanged on a tree."* Ephesians 1:7 is also clear that *"In him [Jesus] we have redemption through his blood, the forgiveness of sins, in accordance with the riches of God's grace."* Here again, it is also clear that the riches of God's grace come to us via the Cross. Acts 2:38 tells us how we get the blood of Jesus to work for us.

Justification

Someone defines justification as a divine declaration that a person is innocent of sin and is now righteous in God's eyes. Romans 3:22-24 says *"This righteousness is given through faith in Jesus Christ to all who believe. There is no difference between Jew and Gentile, for all have sinned and fall short of the glory of God, and all are justified freely by his grace through the redemption that came by Christ Jesus."* Don't be misled by the reference in the above verse to "faith in Jesus to all who believe" because elsewhere in the Bible we are told we should believe and be baptized [Mark 16:16] to be saved.

Note here that all these verses I am using to make my point apply to every Christian who has been baptized by full immersion without exception. They do not apply to people who have been 'fake' baptized or those who believe they are saved by grace alone through faith. There is no such thing without baptism[23]. The Church is fully aware of this, that's why they introduced fake baptisms to make you believe you too have been baptized. These tricks by the Church are designed to lull you into believing you too have been baptized. The question is why does the Church try so hard to avoid the real thing? Jesus was baptized by full immersion, why not you?

Sanctification

To sanctify a person is to make that person holy. The Dictionary says the action or process of being freed from sin or purified. To sanctify something is to set it apart for God's special use and purpose *"Or do you not know that wrongdoers will not inherit the kingdom of God? Do not be deceived: Neither the sexually immoral nor idolaters nor adulterers nor men who have sex with men, nor thieves nor the greedy nor drunkards nor slanderers nor swindlers will inherit the kingdom of God. And that is what some of you were. But you were washed, you were sanctified, you were justified in the name of the Lord Jesus Christ and by the Spirit of our God."*

Note here that marriage between a man and a woman solves the sexual immoral part of this puzzle, while baptism by full immersion solves everything. You are now washed clean of all these sins. So, what are you waiting for, get up and get baptized so you too can partake in his grace, the grace that comes to you via the cross.

23

Rapture

One can search the Bible all they want but they will not find the word "rapture" in it. The word is used today to mean the second coming of the Lord Jesus. There are several verses in the Bible on this subject, and 1 Thessalonians 4:16-17 is the most succinct of them all. It says, *"For the Lord himself will come down from heaven, with a loud command, with the voice of the archangel and with the trumpet call of God, and the dead in Christ will rise first. After that, we who are still alive and are left will be caught up together with them in the clouds to meet the Lord in the air. And so we will be with the Lord forever."*

If you study the above topics closely, you will soon realize that they are all linked to Jesus Christ and his death on the Cross. This last quoted passage uses the term 'the dead in Christ' to refer to those who have died in Christ. All these people barring any miracles, received that one baptism of the Bible. What your pastors are hiding from you is that you cannot partake in any of these blessings without first being baptized by full immersion, according to the Bible.

The false prophet has thus convinced many Christians to believe they too are baptized by giving them a fake baptism and that therefore they too are 'in Christ'. One way to confirm you have been misled is to do a Web search for a list of Bible verses on baptism and see if they all apply to you. All verses on baptism should apply to you if you have been baptized by full immersion. Try this litmus test.

My top Bible verses on baptism are:

Matthew 28:16-20	The Great Commission
Mark 16:15-16	Ditto
Acts 2:38-41	Repent and be baptized
Ephesians 4:4-6	There is one baptism
Galatians 3:27	Have you been baptized into Christ [listen to the Bible]

Romans 6:1-4	United with Jesus through baptism
Colossians 2:9-13	Similar – we are buried with Christ in baptism
Acts 1:4-5	John baptized with water, you will be baptized w/Holy Spirit
1 Cor 12:12-13	In one Spirit, we were baptized into one body
W Peter 3:18-22	Compares Noah's Ark saving to Jesus saving us thru baptism
Acts 22:16	Why wait, rise and be baptized
1 Thes 4:16-17	The dead in Christ

There are probably 30 more verses like the ones above. If you were baptized by full immersion like the Lord Jesus and the Ethiopian eunuch were, all these verses should apply to you without exception. If you were fake baptized or have been led to believe that 'faith alone in Jesus through God's grace saves you' without baptism, then think again. None of the verses on baptism apply to you. The only reason you believe these verses and their promises apply to you is because you have been led to believe that by your church. You believed a lie, which means you were deceived.

These churches preach that your counterfeit baptism is just as good as the real thing but if I have convinced you that there is only one baptism [Ephesians 4:4-6], and that baptism is only by full immersion [Matthew 3:16-17; Acts 8:38-41], and that man- made baptisms do not baptize, I am sure you now know what to do next. Go and get yourself baptized the right way [Acts 22:16]. When you take that one step, all these verses and promises of the New Testament will apply to you too. This whole debate about baptism will suddenly be in your rear-view mirror forever.

As of now however, you're still under the Law of Moses or whatever other belief system your ancestors had before Christ. Romans 2:14-16 alludes to that when it says *"Indeed, when Gentiles, who do not have the law, do by nature things required by the law, they are a law for themselves, even though they do not have the law. So they show that the work of the law is written on their hearts, their consciences also bearing witness, and their thoughts either accusing or defending them on the day when God will judge men's secrets through Christ Jesus, as proclaimed by my gospel."* Even though your pastor will not tell you so, what I am telling you is the Bible truth. We can now formulate a question for our $30,000 Book Challenge, and that question is: By what miracle did you escape from being under the law of Moses to being under the new covenant with Jesus Christ without baptism by full immersion?

BOOK II
[INFORMATIONAL]

CHAPTER 6

BORN AGAIN CHRISTIANITY

Acts 2:14-41 is our guide to becoming born-again Christians.

The term born again itself is not precisely defined in the Bible. We therefore must look elsewhere in the Bible to decipher the correct meaning of the term. This much we know. Jesus was the author of the term in the New Testament.

In John 3:3-5, Jesus is speaking to Nicodemus, a high-ranking Pharisee of his time.

He tells him one cannot enter the kingdom of God without being born again. Our entry into heaven is therefore conditioned on our being born again. Since every Christion I know wants to go to heaven, we need to know exactly how one is born again.

When Nicodemus responded that one cannot be born twice, Jesus made it clear this second birth had nothing to do with a mother's womb but was a spiritual birth. He said in John 3:5, *"Very truly I tell you, no one can enter the kingdom of God unless they are born of water and the Spirit."*

The key question to be asked here is what did Jesus mean by that term born again? That is the question Christianity has been trying to answer ever since. It is not because the Bible is ambiguous about the term. The apostles who succeeded Jesus in his ministry had no doubt what Jesus meant. To them, it meant baptism by full immersion. This is the baptism they practiced even after Jesus ascended to heaven.

God shows us the baptism of the Ethiopian eunuch to bring this message home. If you imitate this baptism, you cannot be wrong about your status as a born again Christian.

That baptism was however inconvenient for the apostate Catholic Church that came into existence early in the 4th century under Constantine the Great. An infusion of a pagan priesthood into the church led to a relaxation of religious beliefs and practices inherited from the apostles and early church fathers. The Sabbath changed from Saturday to Sunday. That much we know, because we live it. Baptism was relaxed as well to accommodate the practice of pouring and sprinkling. We know this change was underway as early as the 4th century because that must be how Constantine was baptized when he died in 337 AD. History records that he was baptized on his deathbed.

I say every Christian needs to know everything there is to know about baptism and what it means for one to be born again because we all expect to go to heaven when we die. Nobody wants to end up in that other place [hell] when they die. Yet for centuries now, there is still no clarity on this issue even though Acts 2:38 is clear what we need to do to be saved. The apostle Peter told the people gathered on the day of Pentecost to *"Repent and be baptized, every one of you, in the name of Jesus Christ for the forgiveness of your sins. And you will receive the gift of the Holy Spirit."* The verse, including the apostle's preceding teaching on that day, gave us five steps:

1. We hear the good news about Jesus Christ, and if

2. We believe what we hear,

3. We repent, and

4. We are baptized for the forgiveness of our sins, and when we do that,

5. We receive the gift of the Holy Spirit.

Let us now go back and re-read John 3:16 that tells us those who believe in God's only begotten son will not perish. What exactly did

God mean. Which 'saved' does God have in mind here because in Mark 16:16 and Matthew 28:19-20 along with Acts 2:38 we see how all these verses reinforce the need for us to be baptized after we believe. Mark 16:16 tells us those who believe and are baptized will be saved, and the words of the apostle in Acts 2:38 are unambiguous and undisputed.

The only issue that confuses people is what the apostle in Acts 2:38 means by the words 'be baptized' in this passage. We showed the answer in a previous chapter by going to the definition of the Greek word 'baptizo' and what the word meant to people in Jesus' time. It meant one being fully submerged in water, and the baptisms of Jesus and that of the eunuch confirm that.

Our second challenge is to factor into this analysis Ephesians 4:4-6 which says there is only one baptism. We already answered that question. We said the one baptism of Ephesians 4:4-6 cannot be different from the baptism of Jesus Christ and of the eunuch. They were both baptized by full immersion. His apostles submitted to this same baptism. People were fully submerged in water and used this same baptism in their ministry.

As I said, we get confirmation of that in Acts 8:38-39 when the Ethiopian eunuch is baptized by one of these apostles. Philip went into the water with the eunuch and baptized him, and when that exercise was completed, the apostle miraculously disappeared. The Bible says God took him away. So, God was present during that baptism.

Unless therefore we are denying that the eunuch's baptism was complete, we cannot argue that after his baptism he was not saved or a born-again Christian.

However, the modern Christian church is not in full agreement with that in practice. It has departed from this Christian baptism of the Bible. We have already seen what the Catholic Church has to say about baptism, and it's worth repeating here.

In its Catechism, paragraph 1239, it says *"Baptism properly speaking. It signifies and actually brings about death to sin and entry into the life of the Most Holy Trinity through configuration of the Paschal mystery of Christ Baptism is performed in the most expressive way by triple immersion in the baptismal water. However, from ancient times it has also been able to be conferred by pouring the water three times over the candidate's head."*

This statement represents a clear departure from what the Bible teaches. It is also a clear admission by the Church of its own noncompliance with the Bible on baptism. What the Church will not tell you is that while imitating Jesus in baptism does baptize, meaning your sins are washed away (forgiven), and you receive the gift of the Holy Spirit, their practices in baptism do not. When you follow the Bible, you're truly born again when you're baptized. You've received a new birth, a spiritual birth and you're now a new creation in Christ Jesus (2 Corinthians 5:17).

But does the Church's preferred baptism of pouring (or sprinkling) bring about this spiritual rebirth of the Bible? My simple answer to that is 'No'. It doesn't. For starters, it is a man-made baptism and therefore not biblical. It is of the Antichrist because it prevents more than half of all Christians from entering the kingdom of God, if we go by John 3:3. Secondly, there is no evidence we receive the Holy Spirit when water is poured or sprinkled on us to symbolize baptism.

One could argue here that there is no evidence we receive the Holy Spirit when we are baptized by full immersion either. Fair enough, but faith in Jesus Christ means we trust everything he has taught us to be true. Remember that the Bible defines faith as believing and trusting Jesus. The Amplified Bible renders this definition as Yet every Christian I know who has not submitted to the one baptism of the New Testament also believes they have received the gift of the Holy Spirit. They believe they have been united with Jesus in his death and resurrection through baptism, etc., even though some have not even gone through a baptism, fake or real. How foolish is that? the Bible gives us the answer. 2 Corinthians 4:4 tells us *"The god of this age has blinded the minds of unbelievers, so that they cannot see the light of the gospel that displays the glory of Christ, who is the image of God."*

We can conclude from everything we have read in the New Testament that (1) according to the Christian Bible, baptism is by full immersion, (2) there is only one baptism, and (3) churches that do not baptize by full immersion are out of step with the Bible. They are disobedient to God's command in the Great Commission [Matthew 28:19-20] to evangelize and baptize the converted. While counterfeit baptisms have fooled many, the practice cannot be reconciled with the one baptism of the Bible. There is either one or more than one baptism, and as Christians, we are taught that the Bible is the inspired word of God. In this regard, God says there is one baptism, one God, one Spirit, etc. These churches that do otherwise, clearly disagree with the truth of the Bible on the issue of baptism.

The Catholic Church for one has had a role to play in creating this situation and admits it. It pays lip service to biblical baptism [New Testament] but offers its congregants something different. It offers pouring and/or sprinkling instead. The question that should be directed to the Pope is: Does God approve of these man-made practices? Chances are the Pope cannot quite answer that question either because he too is a victim of the lie about baptism he inherited or he has also bought into the lie. He inherited a corrupted religious system that has done a lot of good in spreading the gospel of Jesus, in education and in delivering health services worldwide, yet the system he heads is spiritually, a fraud.

So, let's go back to what the Apostle Peter said in Acts 2:38 and ask the question - what did the Apostle mean by telling us we must be baptized? If there is only one baptism, which baptism was he talking about? I have already answered these questions in previous chapters. We know of course that he was talking about the baptism of John the Baptist, the baptism of Jesus Christ, and the baptism of the Ethiopian eunuch. All these baptisms were by full immersion in water. We should therefore safely conclude that baptism by full immersion must be the baptism of the Christian Bible, which we have done.

Every Christian who has followed this Acts 2:38 script must have received a spiritual rebirth that Jesus had in mind when he said we cannot enter the kingdom of God without this rebirth. Those who have followed the Acts 2:38 script must be truly born again, and as I have shown above, even the all-mighty Catholic Church does not disagree with that.

So, how come more than half of all Christians believe they are born again when they have not been baptized by full immersion? That unfortunately is the million- dollar question I am trying to get you to answer here. Has the Church misled you into believing that contrary to what the Bible teaches, there is another baptism that saves? Has the Church convinced you that the Bible cannot be trusted? If the Lord Jesus has said you cannot enter the kingdom of God (heaven) without being born again, why are you doubting his words?

The only reason that these false prophets can give is Jesus did not mean baptism when he said we should be born-again. I have already exposed that argument as a sham [Chapter 3]. The question we should be asking as Christians is who should we believe on this issue, the Church or the Lord Jesus Christ? As I said in the Introduction, many Christians wrestle with this simple question – am I born again? But only Christians who have not imitated Jesus in baptism should wrestle with that question.

When we ask these people why the confusion and uncertainty about baptism, we get a variety of answers, and they all revolve around church tradition, doctrine, and practice. The Church has been exceptionally successful in misleading previous generations about baptism. They got them, and us as well, believing that we have been baptized even though water was only poured or sprinkled on us.

Likewise, we were led to believe that we will die 'In Christ' [see next chapter] when that cannot be possible if one has not been united with Christ through baptism [Romans 6:3-4]. That baptism was by full immersion. It is therefore necessary for us to reiterate that according to the Christian Bible (1) baptism is by full immersion (2) it washes away our sins (3) we receive the gift of the Holy Spirit (4) we are born again when we are baptized by full immersion [water and the Spirit], and (5) we will die in Christ.

The primary variable in all this is of course how one was baptized. The unanswered question for you child of God is what will happen to you if you die without submitting to that one baptism of the Bible, and if it turns out, that God does not accept your baptism of pouring or sprinkling?

Where do you end up?

There are no second chances; there are no do overs.

CHAPTER 7

Dying In Christ

*For the Lord himself will come down from heaven, with a loud command, with the voice of the archangel and with the trumpet call of God, and **the dead in Christ** will rise first.*

1 Thessalonians 4:16

At many Christian funerals I have attended, the pastors talk about the person being buried as having died "In Christ". This goes on even in churches that do not baptize by full immersion at all. If you have followed my argument this far, only people baptized by full immersion can die "In Christ".

Christians baptized by pouring and sprinkling can only die 'in the Church', but 'not "In Christ" and will not enter the kingdom of God if the Bible is to be believed (John 3:3). Making people not properly baptized believe they are going to heaven is unconscionable and is part of the deception by the Church that needs to be reversed.

The question of course is:

Is it true that every professing Christian who dies without a proper baptism will not enter the kingdom of God? The answer as we have seen is found in John 3:3 and 3:5 where Jesus says, 'unless we are born again of water and the Spirit, we will not see the kingdom of God'. The only chance that this is not so is if one can make the argument based on the Bible that by born again of water and the Spirit Jesus was not talking about baptism by full immersion. The first one to make that argument based on the Christian Bible stands to win big because that is one of the questions to be addressed in my $30,000 Book Challenge.

The key to answering this question lies in accurately defining the term born again as used by the Lord Jesus Christ. If you need to be born again to enter the kingdom of God, it follows according to our 'one baptism' scripture that you need to be baptized (Acts 2:38 and Mark 16:16) by this one baptism of the Christian Bible. We already discussed Ephesians 4:4-6 which tells us there is one baptism. That baptism must be the only baptism found in the Christian Bible [New Testament], and all available evidence points to that baptism being by full immersion. You are invited to challenge my understanding of that verse as well as part of the book challenge.

When Jesus was pressed to explain the meaning of the term 'born again', he unfortunately, did not clarify the issue by saying we should be baptized. Instead, he deepened the mystery by saying 'one should be born (again) of water and the Spirit'. As my argument goes, if by 'water and the Spirit', Jesus meant baptism by full immersion, then your loved one, who was baptized by pouring, sprinkling or through infant baptism, like Pope Francis was, will not enter the kingdom of heaven, unless of course, they have secretly been baptized by full immersion as well.

Of all the Christian luminaries of our time, the Reverend Billy Graham is one of the few to openly admit to being baptized by full immersion, in addition to being christened as a baby. If Jesus is to be believed, therefore, that means all these people who have not been baptized by full immersion will not enter the kingdom of God. Are you willing to take that chance if indeed you're a professing Christian? The irony of this situation is most of us love to swim. We swim in our pools, in rivers, in lakes, in the sea, in the ocean, etc., yet we spend a whole lifetime of Christianity avoiding a simple two-minute ritual that can be done in the privacy of your backyard swimming pools. Baptism by full immersion is that simple, Child of God!

Is it possible that while pastors who are in the know freely dispense fake baptisms to their congregants, they themselves have quietly received the only baptism that baptizes, and that baptism is by full immersion. I already mentioned the Reverend Billy Graham. But to his credit, he was not a hypocrite. He shared his good news with everyone. Make it your duty to know which baptism your pastor received and be surprised. If they preach and practice pouring, sprinkling and infant baptism but privately they have hedged their bets by imitating Jesus in baptism, you know what you're dealing with. Is it very possible that people like Pope Francis, Archbishop Justin Welby, etc., have done the same thing as Billy Graham? I have no idea, but it cannot hurt to ask them!

If Christianity is about the Bible being the inspired word of God, anyone who strays from that principle is in error. If Christianity is about all Christians going to heaven when the die, then be advised that baptism is not a matter of choice but is commanded by God [Matthew 28:16-20; Mark 16:15-16 & Luke 24:44-53]. It is therefore something for us to obey. We need to appreciate the likely consequences of disobeying this particular command.

The Lord Jesus commanded the Apostles 'to teach us believers to obey everything he commanded'. In the context of John 3:3-5, that means if we fail to obey his command that we should be baptized, we will not enter the kingdom of God. It means we will not go to heaven. It is that simple. And please do not misunderstand me, that baptism is by full immersion is understood and practiced by many churches today. This book is directed at those churches that do otherwise and therefore are disobeying God.

Incidentally, I read somewhere that Billy Graham's son, Franklin Graham, who is considered a leader among evangelicals was baptizing somewhere in Alaska in 2020 by full immersion. He is clearly setting a good example for the rest of us. But shouldn't people like him be sounding the alarm about this centuries-old Christian deception.

All that I am arguing about baptism is of course predicated on the Bible being the inspired word of God, on Jesus being who he says he is, and that there is a heaven and hell up there, somewhere. The reason Christians want to be born again is so they can go to heaven when they die. They want to 'die in Christ' and be 'raptured' when Jesus returns to take his church with him. The Bible says, "*… Blessed are those who die in the Lord from now on. Yes, says the Spirit, they are blessed indeed, for they will rest from their hard work; for their good deeds follow them![24]*" (NLT)

In this connection, our challenge is to establish the true meaning of the phrase 'to die in the Lord' or 'the dead in Christ' so nobody is left in any doubt about the truth. We do that by reference to the Bible of course, specifically, to the New Testament, where the terms are found. We are looking for context, but in this case, though the term 'to die in the Lord' is used in Revelation, it is not defined there.

We are looking for a passage in the Bible that gives us the meaning. We therefore must look elsewhere, and we find the term again used in Galatians 3:26-28 among other places. It says, *"So in Christ Jesus, you are all children of God through faith, for all of you who were <u>baptized</u> into Christ have clothed yourselves with Christ. There is neither Jew nor Gentile, neither slave nor free, nor is there male and female, for you are all one in Christ Jesus."*

This one verse summarizes for us this discussion in one sentence. Study what it says for yourself. Spend a day just researching this one verse, and you will not regret it. It says, in Christ Jesus, we are all children of God, through faith. Faith is one of the most abused yet misunderstood words in the Bible. It is a result of being baptized in Christ because we clothe ourselves with Christ so his precious blood shed on the cross can start working for us. It protects us. It heals us.

Appendix III is a list of what the blood of Jesus does for believers who have been baptized by full immersion, i.e., imitated Jesus in baptism.

It should be clear to all that once baptized into Christ, you have clothed yourself with Christ, that you're 'in Christ' and therefore will

---

[24] Revelation 14:13

die 'in Christ'. I also quoted 1 Thessalonians 4:16 above where we find the term 'the dead in Christ'. So, the Bible does address the question directly.

I have already asked the question 'which baptism' and identified baptism by full immersion as the only baptism of the Christian Bible? My challenge to you if you have not been baptized by full immersion is, what makes you believe you've been baptized according to the Bible, if you did not receive that one baptism of the Christian Bible. It is clearly the Church that is behind it all, isn't it? Yet we all know that the Bible truth is that baptism by full immersion is the one baptism of the New Testament. It is the one baptism that brings us into Christ. We know we are 'in Christ' and will die in Christ because the Bible tells us so, and we trust the inspired word of God. We have faith in Jesus. If it says if we are baptized by the one baptism of the Christian Bible, and that baptism was by full immersion, we will be saved, we believe that to be so by faith.

Romans 8:9 says *"You, however, are not in the realm of the flesh but are in the realm of the Spirit, if indeed the Spirit of God lives in you. And if anyone does not have the Spirit of Christ, they do not belong to Christ."* Ask yourself this simple question: Does the Spirit of God live in you, and if so, how did it get there without the one baptism of the Bible?

The apostle Peter told us on Pentecost that we receive the gift of the Holy Spirit at baptism. How then do you accept the lie that you have the Spirit of God in you if you were never baptized in the first place? You are in that situation child of God because you have accepted the lie that pouring and sprinkling also baptize. You have been deceived and you can free yourself from this deception by simply making sure you are baptized the proper way. It's that simple.

The irony of all this is that the same Apostle Paul who wrote the verses in the New Testament referencing baptism is making the same point this book is trying to make, and that is, without baptism [by full immersion], you cannot be 'In Christ'. The false prophet quotes the same verses from Paul's epistles and twists them out of context to mislead the f lock.

As I have said above, we know the Spirit of God lives in us because we were baptized, and the Bible tells us so. That is the faith part in any religion. Faith, according to the Bible is *"confidence in what we hope for, and assurance about what we do not see[25]."* Our whole belief system as Christians is based on faith; faith that God exists, that there is a heaven and hell, and that when we die, we will go to heaven.

Nobody has ever seen this place, yet we believe it exists.

Why?

Because Jesus told us so.

Nowhere else in the Bible [except maybe in Acts 10:47, which I will discuss below], does it tell us there is another way to receive the gift of the Holy Spirit other than through baptism? The Church has misled many into believing *"If you declare with your mouth, "Jesus is Lord," and believe in your heart that God raised him from the dead, you will be saved[26].* There is no such thing in the Bible if this 'saved' means one will be born again. For that 'saved', baptism is required.

Again, it should be clear that you cannot be in Christ if you do not have the Spirit of God in you, and you do not have the Spirit of God in you if you were never baptized. As I said before, the Church has been able to maintain this deception by inventing pseudo-baptisms to lull you into believing that you too have been baptized when they pour or sprinkle water on you. It is an illusion, child of God. The Bible truth is that there are no other baptisms out there except baptism by full immersion.

That is one of our challenge questions of course. We want your pastor, your small Bible study group, or prayer group, your Church as a whole, etc., to address that challenge question, i.e., is the Bible verse [Ephesians 4:4-6] that says there is only one baptism a lie? If it is not a lie, which

---

[25] Hebrews 11:1
[26] Romans 10:9

one is that one baptism and why do you accept church practices that use more than one baptism?

There is another verse we must introduce here because it is also relevant. I said, one reason why we need to be baptized is because we want to be raptured as part of the Lord Jesus' church when he returns. Here is what the Lord Jesus has said on the subject: *"My Father's house has many rooms; if that were not so, would I have told you that I am going there to prepare a place for you? And if I go and prepare a place for you, I will come back and take you to be with me that you also may be where I am. You know the way to the place where I am going*[27]*.* This passage gives us an idea of where we are headed as Christians when we are 'raptured' at the end of the age. We go to heaven.

The church that denies believers a proper baptism is therefore denying them this promise of eternity with our Maker in heaven. These Churches who tell people that they have the spirit of God in them without explaining how this accident or miracle could have happened without baptism (by full immersion) according to Acts 2:38 are misleading the f lock. These people owe us an explanation, and the best way to do so is by them entering our $30,000 Book Challenge and prove this narrative wrong. We therefore need to put the pressure on them to tell the truth. After all, the Bible tells us God is Spirit, and that we should worship him in spirit and truth.

Another argument used by false prophets about the Spirit of God indwelling you without baptism revolves around the baptism of Cornelius and his household in Acts 10:47. They will argue this is the other possible way the Holy Spirit might enter you without baptism. It is the only known exception in the New Testament. We will look at that story more closely, but before doing so, let me warn you upfront that even in that case, a water baptism was required to seal that miracle, so don't fall for that one either.

The verse in question says, *"Surely no one can stand in the way of their being baptized with water. They have received the Holy Spirit just as we*

---

[27] John 14:2

have.[28] ” They will use this verse as evidence you can get the Holy Spirit to come and indwell you without baptism. Unfortunately for these folks, people who make this false argument cannot use it to support the proposition that water baptism is not necessary for salvation, because there was a water baptism in Cornelius's case.

On this occasion, God was present. He was in control. You cannot limit God. He has the power to forgive your sins without the ritual of a baptism for the forgiveness of sins. He did it before with the thief on the cross (Luke 23:39-43). In this case, He was teaching the Apostle Peter and the Jews with him something new; that while the ministry of Jesus was first and foremost to the Jews, after his crucifixion, the ministry had now been expanded to include the Gentiles as well. God poured His Spirit on these Gentiles (re: Cornelius and his household), in a sense, to force Peter to baptize them.

We always need to remember that God alone has the power to forgive sins. He must have done exactly that to allow the Holy Spirit to come and indwell Cornelius and his household. In short, God forced Peter's hand by reversing the order of conversion to Christianity. Instead of a water baptism preceding the arrival of the Holy Spirit, God poured his Spirit on them first. This was and remains an isolated event and should be looked at as such. As I just said above a similar occurrence took place when Jesus forgave the thief on the cross. He did that because he has the power to do so and used that power on that occasion to forgive the thief. That power was however never passed on to the apostles or to the church Jesus founded.

So, let no one be confused by what happened here. The normal order of conversion is that baptism in water brings about baptism with the Spirit and fire (the Holy Spirit) as explained in Acts 2:38. Yes, the baptism of John the Baptist was only for the forgiveness of sins (Mark 1:4). It did not bring about the indwelling of the Holy Spirit because Jesus had not died yet. Under the new covenant with Jesus however, the

---

[28] Acts 10:47

two, i.e., water baptism and the arrival of the Holy Spirit, now happen simultaneously as we saw in the baptism of the Ethiopian eunuch.

There is a question out there in some Christian circles whether baptism in water a separate event from baptism with the Holy Spirit? That issue should also be addressed here as part of our $30,000 Book Challenge. We want to hear from you and your pastor how this Spirit of God came to indwell you without the water baptism of the Bible. The deception the church uses here is to claim that the man-made practices of pouring or sprinkling water on you bring about the same results as baptism by full immersion. However, that is not biblical at all. These practices do not baptize, at least, not according to the Christian Bible.

As I pointed out before, people like Pope Francis, were christened as babies, and so were most of us who were born into Christian families. That however does not preclude the requirement of a proper baptism at the right age. The apostate Christian church of today now calls christening, a baptism to further confuse you. The practice does not meet the other requirements of a Christian baptism. According to Acts 2:38 we (1) hear the good news of Jesus, and (b) believe in Jesus Christ, and then we are (3) baptized. Babies are not capable of hearing the Good News about Jesus and making the decision to become believers. Yet today's Christian babies are somehow supposed to do this according to the Church.

The thing I want you to bear in mind throughout is that even in the case of Cornelius a water baptism was still required. The Bible says in this connection, *"While Peter was still speaking these words, the Holy Spirit came on all who heard the message. The circumcised believers who had come with Peter were astonished that the gift of the Holy Spirit had been poured out even on Gentiles. For they heard them speaking in tongues and praising God. Then Peter said, "Surely no one can stand in the way of their being baptized with water. They have received the Holy Spirit just as we have."* So, he ordered that they be baptized in the name of Jesus Christ. Then they asked Peter to stay with them for a few days."

That this was unusual is conveyed to us by the surprise expressed by the Apostle and the other Jews with him. The Apostle had to baptize Cornelius and his household to seal their salvation. The people being misled by this false argument are the victims of the churches that masquerade as the angels of light when they are nothing but agents of darkness. Their victims are left without a proper baptism and therefore remain unsaved even though they are 'in the church' and believe they are saved.

We were however forewarned about this development by the Lord Jesus when he said that the Pharisees and teachers of the law who were misleading the f lock were shutting the door to heaven of people who wanted to enter. The message here is clear; if you allow yourself to be misled, you too will suffer the same consequences as the culprits who do the misleading. You too will be shut out of heaven.

That statement by Jesus was very prophetic.

Finally, the assumption some of these charlatans make that by household in the Cornelius verse God meant that children were also baptized on this occasion might not be correct. First, we do not know if there were children in this household. The Bible does not say that. So, it is sheer speculation.

Secondly, to believe this is to make the Bible contradict itself because elsewhere the Bible tells us one has to first hear the good news about Jesus and believe (Acts 2:26-38) to make the decision to be baptized. Children cannot do that. Thirdly, even if children had been baptized along with the adults, their baptism would not have met all the other requirements of a valid baptism. They could not have heard the good news about Christ, they had no sins to confess, and lacked the capacity to believe in anything.

CHAPTER 8

Catholic Inf luence on Christianity

I have already touched on this subject in Chapter 2, but it is worth repeating.

The Catholic Church, after it was taken over by Constantine early in the 4th century, had its own ideas about Christianity, the Sabbath, and baptism. We now worship on Sunday instead of Saturday, which is God's Sabbath because the Church made that decision, not God. Our disobedience of the 4th Commandment is clear and complete. While Jesus and his Apostles worshipped on Saturday, we all [except a few] worship on Sunday, a man-made law. It followed Constantine's decree of 7 March 321 AD, changing the day of rest from Saturday to Sunday. His decree said:

> *"All judges and city people and the craftsmen shall rest upon the venerable day of the sun. Country people, however, may freely attend to the cultivation of the fields, because it frequently happens that no other days are better adapted for planting the grain in the furrows or the vines in trenches. So that the advantage given by heavenly providence may not for the occasion of a short time perish."*

YES, the history of that change has a date, 7 March 321 AD. Over the centuries, that change has become institutionalized. We rarely question that anymore, but God's Day of rest remains the 7th day of the week, not the 1st day of the week.

This whole drama came about because Constantine wanted to merge his pagan religious order into the Catholic Church to unite his Roman Empire under one religion. His pagan religious order was the trojan horse that transformed the Catholic Church into what it is today. The problem he wanted to solve was that 90% of his subjects worshipped their sun god on Sunday. It was easier therefore to get Christians, who constituted only 10% of the population to change their day of rest to Sunday. It made political sense to get the Church to change its day of rest to align with the majority, the pagans, but in God's eyes, that was disobedience.

The new church that emerged from merging Constantine's pagan religious order and the Church founded by the Lord Jesus was renamed the Roman Catholic Church in 339 AD. Notice the inclusion of "Catholic Church" in the new organization. That was not by accident child of God, but that was necessary to maintain the illusion of continuity from the Founder of the Church, the Lord Jesus Christ.

The move was purely political of course on the part of Constantine. Henceforth, anything the Church did that did not benefit Constantine politically, he caused the Church to discard. The first to be discarded was, as I said, the Saturday Sabbath. He persuaded the Catholic bishops to go along with his disobedience of the 4th commandment, and the bishops acquiesced. They went ahead and issued their now infamous statement that *"All things whatsoever that it was the duty to do on the Sabbath, these we have transferred to the Lord's Day as more honorable than the Jewish Sabbath.[29]"* This is as good an example as any, of a man-made rule being used by the Church to override God's command.

When there was resistance to the Emperor's edict of 7 March, 321 AD, which decreed that the day of rest would henceforth be Sunday instead of Saturday, the Church issued its also now infamous Canon 29 that told believers *"Christians must not judaize by resting on the <u>Sabbath</u>, but must work on that day, rather honouring the <u>Lord's Day</u>; and, if they can, resting then as <u>Christians</u>. But if any shall be found to be judaizers,*

---

[29] [Parker, John D., The Sabbath Transferred, 1902, pages 93-94

let them be <u>anathema</u> from Christ." Suddenly, God's Day of Rest had a surname, it was now Jewish.

In the eyes of the Church, therefore, those who continued to obey God's fourth commandment were now anathema to Jesus Christ. The Cambridge dictionary tells us the word anathema means "something that is strongly disliked or disapproved'.

How can obeying God be strongly disliked or disapproved, and by who? Not by the Jesus who is 'the same yesterday, today and forever'? It was clearly the devil talking, telling Christians through the Church that if they continued to obey the original Jesus (God) regarding His Sabbath, they would be anathema to the Church's new Jesus, the one who now worshipped on Sunday, and was prepared to disobey God, the Father of the original Jesus Christ, when it suited him.

This goes to show that Canon 29, though it remains on the books of the Catholic Church to this day, is absolute nonsense to the ears of a true believer. To me, it represents the final divorce decree between the original Jesus and his bride, the Church. However, because the Church and the state at the time had the power to enforce these rules and make them stick, the decision became the order of the day. The two institutions, i.e., the state and the Church, together controlled everything and for centuries, ruled the world.

Another factor contributing to this situation and making this possible was that not everyone had access to the Bible at that time. Only the clergy, scholars and the privileged had access to a Bible, making it difficult, if not impossible for the ordinary Christian to fight back. But even if they had, reading it and understanding everything in it was not enough to stand up to the bishops. It was nigh impossible.

Today, we can stand up to the Pope and the Archbishops of our Christian world because technology now allows us to research and confront the powers that be with the truth, the results of our own research. We can list all verses in the Bible that touch on a given topic and quickly assess the truthfulness of what we are being told by the

Church establishment. Things were different then. As I said, only scholars could do the type of in-depth research needed, at a level deep enough to rebut the clerics. The issue of the Sabbath for example was easy to rebut, but who dared to go against the wishes of the emperor, when to do so could open one to possible death or excommunication?

Secondly, Constantine's patronage of the Church was enough to silence the bishops. They had been given the Lateran Palace in 313 AD and were promised a donation of a piece of land on which Constantine was to build St. Peter's Basilica for the Church. We know that piece of land today as the Vatican, the present home of the Roman Catholic Church. In addition to these gifts, a provision was made in the state budget to support Church buildings.

As the lines between the Church and the state became blurred, it was easy to politicize the Sabbath issue and make the lie stick. Suddenly, the Saturday Sabbath was only for the Jews (don't Judaize), and the Sunday Sabbath was for everyone else. That the change was a breach of the 10 Commandments, was never addressed by the apostate church of the day. It was not a surprise therefore that once the Church acquiesced to Constantine's demands there was no organized opposition to the change.

Incidentally, the only reason we still worship on Sunday today is because of that decree of 7 March, 321 AD. And as for Canon 29, it is still valid for all Catholics and all Christian denominations who follow the Catholic tradition. They include the Methodists, the Lutherans, the Anglicans, etc., even the Baptists, they also worship on Constantine's day of rest, Sunday.

The apostate Catholic Church under Constantine also moved away from baptizing people as prescribed in the Bible. They started introducing 'fake' baptisms based on the Didache, a document whose authorship remains a mystery to this day. Given that the Roman Catholic Church eventually became the state, this development gave it the power it needed to enforce its 'antichrist' decrees and agenda. The

Catholic tradition has therefore misled many people into believing they are born-again Christians when they are not.

I previously alluded to paragraph 1239 of the Catechism of the Catholic Church (CCC), where the Church said *"The essential right of the sacrament follows: Baptism properly speaking. It signifies and actually brings about death to sin and entering into the life of the most Holy Trinity through configuration through the Paschal mystery of Christ. Baptism is performed in the most expressive way by triple immersion in the baptismal water. However, from ancient times it is also been able to be conferred by pouring the water three times over the candidate's head."*

We are being told here, in clear language, that the original baptism was by triple immersion but that the Roman Catholic Church has developed its own tradition that uses pouring. The question that needs to be answered is, does God accept that man- made tradition? That question is the essence of this book, and of course, nobody living can answer it. I have however shown that the Bible provides an answer, and that answer is no, God does not accept man-made laws to override his word.

So, is a tradition that does not have God's endorsement valid?

Does a tradition that departs from the biblical teaching of baptism by immersion in water have any validity in God's eyes?

Isn't the tradition the Church should follow be that of John the Baptist and Jesus Christ and his Apostles?

Is the Church's new baptism as transformative as the original?

Are your sins washed away and does God's Spirit come to indwell you?

Nobody living can answer these critical questions. So, I ask again the same old question: Are you born again when they pour water three times over your head in this church-inspired ritual of baptism? My answer is of course NO.

What is yours?

Let me tell you again child of God, you are not born again. You're just another professing Christian who has yet to be saved, and you're still under the law of Moses or whatever other religious belief system your pre-Jesus ancestors believed in.

A key question I have asked the Church over and over is this:

If God does not accept this Catholic Church-inspired baptism of pouring and/or sprinkling, what is the fate of those who have been misled into believing man-made baptisms are just as good as the real thing? Where will these people go when they die [John 3:3] if they cannot enter the kingdom of God on account their man-made baptism. The answer to that is they will go to hell.

This suggests that the Church's counterfeit baptisms might be part of a devil-inspired plot to stop you from going to heaven when you die. Get your pastor to answer these questions for you. I know the Pope will not answer this question for you, unless he claims like some of his predecessors did, that he is God on earth, which he is not.

So, what is going to happen to you child of God when you die? Fortunately, the Lord Jesus Christ answered that question for you. He is on record as saying *"Woe to you, teachers of the law and Pharisees, you hypocrites! You shut the door of the kingdom of heaven in people's faces. You yourselves do not enter, nor will you let those enter who are trying to[30]."* If you have not been baptized by full immersion, you're the one trying to go to heaven but is being prevented from doing so by today's Pharisees. Today's Pharisees are the very people giving you a fake baptism, the clergy who according to the Lord Jesus Christ, will themselves not enter the kingdom of God (heaven) either.

These words by Jesus are as valid today as they were when they were first spoken, for the Bible tells us *"… the word of God is alive and active. Sharper than any double-edged sword, it penetrates even to dividing soul and spirit, joints and marrow; it judges the thoughts and attitudes of the heart.[31]"*

---

[30] Matthew 23:13
[31] Hebrews 4:12

Focus therefore on identifying for yourself these people in your own life so you can better fight back. If you are like me, your list will include your pastor, the one who gave you that fake baptism when you did not know any better. It will include your church and all the higher-ups like Pope Francis, Archbishop Justin Welby and their supporting cast, the clergy, who are denying believers the one baptism that saves by teaching falsehoods.

So, child of God, you owe it to yourself to sit down with your pastor and really find out from him/her by what miracle you are going to end up in heaven if you have not fulfilled the very condition the Lord Jesus Christ put on entry into the Kingdom of God [John 3:3-5]. I remind you yet again that he said unless you're born again of water and the Spirit, you cannot enter the Kingdom of God.

So, are you born again?

Do you understand what that term even means?

The Catholic position on this subject stands in stark contrast to scripture. But the Catholics have already told us that the Bible is not their only source of scripture.

That's a great escape on a human level, but not on a spiritual level. These people won't be there with you when you are denied entry into heaven. They are therefore able to escape confronting these facts, i.e., that there is only one baptism, not two, not three, etc., according to Ephesians 4:4-6). That verse, which I keep bringing up for emphasis is clear and conclusive for every Bible-believing Christian and you should be guided by it. It says, *"There is one body and one Spirit, just as you were called to one hope when you were called; one Lord, one faith, **one baptism;** one God and Father of all, who is over all and through all and in all."*

The verse clearly establishes the oneness of everything; one God, the Father of all, one body, one Spirit, one hope, one Lord, one faith and one baptism. How then will the devil inspired forces of our Christian faith argue that there is another baptism other than the one in the Bible, which we have established is by full immersion.

If we are to believe scripture, then the Catholic situation cannot be sustained. They are using two baptisms here and not one. Pouring is their preferred mode of baptizing. Knowing what we now know about God, i.e., in Mark 7:7-13, what should we make of our predicament. That passage in the Bible tells us *"They worship me in vain; their teachings are merely human rules.' You have let go of the commands of God and are holding on to human traditions." And he continued, "You have a fine way of setting aside the commands of God in order to observe your own traditions! For Moses said, 'Honor your father and mother,' and, 'Anyone who curses their father or mother is to be put to death.' But you say that if anyone declares that what might have been used to help their father or mother is Corban (that is, devoted to God) — then you no longer let them do anything for their father or mother. Thus you nullify the word of God by your tradition that you have handed down. And you do many things like that."*

Isn't this exactly what the Catholics and all the other churches in the Catholic tradition have done, and are still doing today? How then do they justify their approach to born-again Christianity based on pouring, sprinkling, and infant baptisms as opposed to baptism by full immersion in the manner of John the Baptist when he baptized the Lord Jesus Christ (Matthew 3:16-17), and the Apostle Philip when he baptized the Ethiopian eunuch (Acts 8:39)?

Finally, what is the effect of offering Christians a fake baptism? Isn't it to deny them the eternity with our Creator that the Bible promises. As an aside, I have often wondered if some of our leaders past and present; people like the late Queen Elizabeth, Prince Phillip, Robert Gabriel Mugabe, etc., and those still living, like Joe Biden, Pope Francis, and Archbishop Justin Welby, Prince Charles, Donald Trump, to name but a few, have not all been secretly baptized by full immersion as a hedge against ending up in hell. After all, we know from the horse's mouth that the Reverend Billy Graham did exactly that, though not secretly.

These people have access to all this information I am sharing in this book. They have swimming pools in their backyards and access to pastors 24/7, so why would they not go the extra mile and be properly baptized as a hedge against ending up in hell?

King Charles is now the head of the Church of England, has he been properly baptized, or was he simply christened as a child, and then confirmed when he reached a certain age.

Listen, I don't want to sound like a present-day John the Baptist, for I am not. I just find myself asking these questions as though I am inspired to do so. I do not speak to God that way, so these words are purely mine, as a mortal being. They are however inspired by the Christian Bible. Just as we take out insurance to mitigate against known risk, one would think that these people have done the same just in case the Church has gotten it all wrong about baptism.

Well, if they have not been properly baptized, and Jesus is who he says he is, they will not see the kingdom of God, and you the baptized will not see them in heaven. No Siree, unless they have secretly gone through the Christian ritual of baptism by full immersion, they will not enter the kingdom of God.

So, says the Lord Jesus Christ (John 3:3-5).

People need to understand that the Pope is not God. He is fallible like you and me, and were all his predecessors. He inherited the system that created the confusion we now have to live with. We can still ask the Church to tell us what our eternal fate will be if it turns out that the Church is wrong about the baptism it is offers that are not in the Bible. We ask these questions because these baptisms are different from the one baptism of the New Testament.

By the simple message of this book, I am also asking every believer to make it their duty to ask their pastors for an explanation for the baptism they received, if that baptism was not by full immersion. If the pastors cannot give a satisfactory answer, then I advise you to ask for an authentic baptism. If they will not oblige you, you should look elsewhere for a church that baptizes. You can also invite your pastor to enter our $30,000 Book Challenge to explain and support their practices in baptism. Everyone, including students in colleges like Concordia, seminary students, etc., are eligible to enter the Challenge individually or in groups.

Ours is a campaign for the billions of Christian souls, dead or alive, that have been misled into believing they have died or will die in Christ when their baptism was through infant baptisms, pouring, and/or sprinkling. At stake here is the eternal fate of all these billions of souls that have been misled.

As children and/or grandchildren of people now approaching the sunset years of their lives, you also have a duty to have an honest discussion with your grannies to make sure if they are Christians, they will die in Christ by getting them properly baptized by full immersion before they die. This is a must if you want to see them again in heaven.

CHAPTER 9

False Prophets and John 3:3-5

There is one body and one Spirit just as you were called to one hope when you were called; one Lord, one faith, one baptism; one God and Father of all, who is over all and through all and in all.

Ephesians 4:4-6

Before tackling this very vexing topic, we need to be clear and observe many biblical constraints here. The first for us to acknowledge is that scripture does not contradict scripture. So, if Ephesians 4:4-6 says there is one baptism and you see two, or more, then something is wrong with you if you are not asking questions.

Anything that departs from the one baptism of the Bible, cannot save.

Secondly, if God says Jesus is our example, anyone who has imitated Jesus in baptism must have satisfied the requirement that we should be born again to enter the kingdom of God. Furthermore, in showing us the baptism of the Ethiopian eunuchs, God reinforced the validity of the 'one' baptism of the Bible in the quoted verse above. The Spirit of God was in attendance during that baptism and guided the process. Those who follow the example of the eunuch in baptism are truly born again and will die in the Lord [Revelation 14:13; Romans 8:1; Romans

6:11]. Those who argue otherwise are the critics of God and of the Bible. Give them no foothold in your Christian life.

Thirdly, the baptism of the Ethiopian eunuch that happened after Pentecost as I said, reinforces the Jesus example in baptism rather than detract from it. Any arguments, seeking to identify a different baptism than full immersion, must overcome this constraint. And fourthly, the literal rule for interpreting the Bible must prevail. Rejecting the literal rule in order to distort the truth of the Bible is used by the antichrist to transform Bible verses into satanic verses. We must reject this. Those engaged in these practices are the charlatans we are waging this war against.

Let us begin.

I read a rather convoluted article from *GotQuestions.org* in which the subject of baptism is discussed. The article was titled *"Does John 3:5 teach that baptism is necessary for salvation?"* First, that is a deceptive heading. That passage teaches only that you cannot enter the kingdom of God unless you are born again of water and the Spirit. The verse that teaches that baptism is necessary for salvation is Mark 16:16. The only issue John 3:5 should raise in anybody's mind is the question, what did Jesus mean by one being born again of water and the Spirit.

It stands to reason that if he meant we should be baptized by full immersion, then, yes, baptism is necessary for salvation. I have argued throughout this book that John 3:3-5 is about baptism by full immersion, and that this is the 'one baptism' of the Christian Bible. The book challenge invites those who disagree to counter my arguments on the basis of the Christian Bible alone. There are several other verses in the Christian Bible that tell us a water baptism is necessary for salvation and they include Mark 16:16, Acts 2:38, Acts 16:30-34 as well as Matthew 28:19, among many others. So, this article is not what it claims to be, but is an attack on John 3:5, an attempt to discredit that verse.

Those who disagree should submit a rebuttal instead. In Acts 16:30, the jailer asks the apostles a direct question: what should I do to be saved? False prophets should address verses like this in the Christian Bible before offering us their unbiblical opinions. Those who do not believe Jesus was talking about baptism by full immersion should focus on that issue instead of making foolish and irrelevant arguments to confuse the issue.

The article went on to make several mistakes in its analysis.

First, it misses the time factor by seeking to use Apostle Paul's writings to negate or supersede what we learned from Jesus' example while he walked the earth, and of course, his statement in John 3:3-5 that we need to be born again of water and the Spirit for salvation. To most of us salvation means entering the kingdom of God. Those who do not believe that Jesus was talking about the one baptism of the Bible should focus on that issue and the Bible provides the answer.

If we examine closely the baptism of the eunuch, it is all there. He says to Philip, "Look, here is some water. What can stand in the way of my being baptized?" Of course, there was nothing that stood in the way of his baptism. Water must have been plentiful, and the eunuch was duly baptized by full immersion following the same script as the one used when Jesus was baptized. He was fulfilling the command by the Lord Jesus in the Great Commission that those who believe should be baptized. That was the same baptism referenced in Mark 16:16, in Acts 2:38 and in Acts 16:30-33.

In the eunuch's case, as was the case when Jesus was baptized, the Bible tells us God was present. So, why do the infidels of our Christian world insist a water baptism is not necessary for salvation? On whose authority are these people operating? Their arguments do contradict the Bible, and that is a no-no.

The reality is that by the time Paul came onto the Christian scene with his epistles, the new covenant with Jesus was at least 25 years old and people were converting to Christianity every day. Were they mistaken by being baptized by full immersion? Of course not. Baptism was always a requirement. Therefore, to argue that salvation is by faith alone contradicts the Bible and using Ephesians 2:8-9 as your authority is to mislead people based on ignorance, if not outright deceit. To accept such an argument would mean that all the people who converted to Christianity and were baptized according to Jesus' command in the Great Commission between Pentecost and the coming of Paul, were all in error, a very unlikely thing indeed. It would mean that Paul's own baptism by Ananias was also in error.

It also means the Apostles who baptized believers by full immersion following the example of John the Baptist and the Lord Jesus Christ had it all wrong. It would mean the baptism of the Ethiopian eunuch as I said above by the Apostle Philip under the guidance of God's Spirit and the accompanying teaching [Acts 8:26-41] were all in error. It would mean that Ephesians 4:4-6 which tells us there is one baptism is also wrong.

That, simply said, cannot be true!

Furthermore, it would mean that all those who converted to Christianity during the first 25 years after Pentecost were misguided and that Jesus' command in the Great Commission is irrelevant, and therefore should be disregarded. That is sheer lunacy, of course, fueled only by sheer ignorance.

The article falsely argues that John 3:16 is clear that salvation is by faith alone. That verse says no such thing at all. That argument implies that believing in Jesus [John 3:16] and having faith in Jesus are one and the same thing, which would be incorrect. The two might be two sides of the same coin but they are not the same. The two verses, John 3:16 and Mark 16:16 make that clear, unless these charlatans are arguing that the Bible has contradicted itself in this instance.

Faith in Jesus is a much broader concept that we demonstrate by obeying the Lord Jesus' command by getting baptized. That is part of having faith in Jesus. One mistake the Church makes is trying to undermine the authority of Mark 16:16 by saying the verse was not in the original draft of the book of Mark. But that verse says the same thing as in the Great Commission. Matthew 28:19-20 and Mark 16:16 are reporting the same event, and both say those who believe should be baptized.

Additionally, the 'grace alone/faith alone' brigade and their arguments do not meet this requirement. Scripture is clear in both Mark and Matthew that those who believe and are baptized will be saved. Believing alone is clearly not enough. We again see this principle demonstrated when the jailer and his household are saved (Acts 16:25-40, especially verses 30 – 34 that starts *"Sirs, what must I do to be saved?"* As I said, the reason people continue to make this mistake is they fail to recognize that Matthew 28:19-20 and Mark 16:16 are reporting the same event in the Bible. It was Jesus giving his final instructions to his disciples before ascending to heaven.

The article also wanders off the mark when it discusses John 3:7 & 8 and brings in the idea of "living water" which it borrows from Jesus' encounter with the Samaritan woman [John 4:10]. This is a good example of grasping at straws to make a point that can otherwise not be sustained. The two events are unrelated.

Finally, one must take issue with references to Ezekiel 36:25-27 in this article. It is not relevant here because nowhere in the New Testament does one see Jesus or his apostles sprinkle water as a means of baptizing believers. What we see are people being dunked in water when they are baptized. So, this reference in the article is unfortunate and can only mislead.

The article says at one point baptism does not save us, which contradicts Mark 16:16 that says those who believe and are baptized will be saved and Acts 16:30-34 that puts that teaching into action. Here, the jailer was told he needed to believe in God to be saved, and after hearing the good news from Paul and Silas, he was baptized.

The conclusion to the article can only be described as bizarre because after writing all this irrelevant stuff, the article then acknowledges the significance of baptism in the process of being saved.

I also read an article in *MyCatholicWill.com/CatholicAnswers* titled *"Born Again – the Bible Way"* by Tim Staples. The article, in typical Catholic gobbledygook. It pays lip-service to the Bible but does not address key Bible verses on the subject. It says, "Yes, I have been born again – when I was baptized," but the author does not identify which baptism he is talking about since Catholics use more than one baptism. If the Bible says there is only one baptism but in practice you use more than one baptism, which one are you referencing in an article like this. Thus, the author, like his church, pays lip service to the need for baptism but does not answer the key question: - **If the bible says there is one baptism, and the Church uses more than one baptism, which baptism is the valid one in the eyes of God?** Which baptism are you talking about?

If Jesus commanded baptism of the converted, and we see his apostles baptizing by full immersion, isn't that then the one baptism of the New Testament? The writer agrees however that John 3:3-5 teaches us about the essential nature of baptism, but again will not identify the baptism he is talking about. This is part of the deception we are fighting, whether this author realizes it or not.

The author is telling us indirectly that pouring, sprinkling, infant baptism and baptism by full immersion are all the same, when only one of them has biblical support. In general, Catholics have been known to use baptism by full immersion, by pouring, by sprinkling, and infant baptism as well, thereby contradicting the one baptism scripture in the New Testament.

The article is correct that John 3:5 is not talking about two events – a water baptism and a Spirit baptism as some charlatans are apt to argue. When one is baptized by full immersion, all these things happen simultaneously. We see that most clearly in the baptism of the Ethiopian eunuch [Acts 8:38-39]. The article then talks about "baptismal water", something we will not find in the Bible, but is primarily descriptive of Catholic practice. Catholics pray for water they then use to pour or sprinkle on the candidate for baptism, a clear departure from the baptism of the Bible. They do not even try to explain away scripture like Ephesians 4:4-6, Romans 6:3-4 and Colossians 2:11-12 in doing so.

One should mention in all fairness that there is now a growing movement within the Catholic and Anglican Churches to baptize by full immersion. The introduction of baptismal pools/fonts in some churches is a concession to this truth. An article by Francis Mannion of May 8, 2015, is instructive on this subject[32]. Those of the Anglican persuasion can read an article by Cara Bentley titled 'Full immersion baptism allowed again in church' posted on August 24, 2020[33]. These articles are a clear admission by the Church that they have been doing baptism all wrong all these centuries, and they are trying to change, but change at the margins is not enough. These churches should make a complete 180 degree turn on baptism.

The Charis movement in the Catholic Church might be the spark that brings about the change we are looking for. Pope Francis is considered a supporter of this movement, and those interested in knowing more should read an article by Austen Ivereigh in America Magazine published June 14, 2019, titled "Is Francis our first charismatic pope?" Charis represents a promise for change in the largest Christian church in the world. In line with scripture, it should come out and mandate baptism by full immersion for all. Even as some of us criticize the Catholic Church and its decadent doctrine, we are not unmindful of its enormous contribution to Christian evangelism, education and health services worldwide. But what good is this when you are misleading many about their baptism and therefore, their eternity?

We should also remember that the Catholics have done the same thing concerning the Sabbath. They changed it from Saturday to Sunday, and proof of their disobedience is in their statement at the time that was made public by the Roman Catholic Church some 18 years

[32] Initiation/RCIA, Viewpoint by Francis Mannion
[33] Anglican Mainstream by Cara Bentley, 24 August, 2020

later in 339 AD. It was crafted by Eusebius, Constantine's Imperial court advisor and said:

All things whatsoever it was duty to do on the Sabbath, we [Eusebius, Constantine, and other Catholic bishops of the time] *have transferred to the Lord's Day* [the 1st day of the week] *as more appropriately belonging to it."*

The Sunday Sabbath is therefore most definitely a man-made law. The question is does God approve of this man-made change? The answer must be a clear No. How do we know this? We know this to be so because Jesus warned us about these deceptions before they happened. In Mark 7:9 we are told *"You have a fine way of setting aside the commands of God in order to observe your own traditions!"* and in Mark 7:13 Jesus continued, *"Thus, you nullify the word of God by your tradition that you have handed down. And you do many things like that."* That was very prophetic of the Lord Jesus Christ for within 300 years of his death, these things started to happen.

CHAPTER 10

Post Biblical Developments in Baptism

Let us now deal brief ly with some post-biblical developments in baptism that have no biblical support. We have already alluded to them. They include infant baptisms, pouring, and sprinkling, of course. Many Christians are unaware that these practices did not exist when Jesus walked the earth. The Catholic Church baptized by full immersion. Then when the pagans came in with Constantine, change started until the Church almost completely abandoned baptism by full immersion. That remained the status quo for some 1300 years.

That Baptism is by full immersion as practiced by John the Baptists, Jesus Christ and the Apostles is not in dispute. Yet for some 1300 years after Constantine took over the church, the Church tended to use pouring and sprinkling to baptize. Baptism by full immersion was only re-introduced to Christianity during the Reformation.

During those 1300 years however, the church tradition of baptizing by pouring reigned supreme. Sprinkling was also practiced by the Church during those years. Infant baptisms only entered the Church during the later part of that period (from about 1100 AD).

Recently, I read a short article titled "On The History and Doctrine of Baptism"[34]. It was eye-opening for me because it highlighted the fact that when the Anabaptists insisted on restoring the original 'one'

---

[34] https://nshorechurch.com

baptism of the New Testament to the Church during Reformation, they were violently attacked and their leaders martyred by being drowned, not just by the Catholics, but also by the reformers, including the Lutherans and Calvinists. The article was a good read for me, and I recommend it to you and others, even though there are things in there I do not necessarily agree with.

To me, baptism is a sacrament, a Christian ritual for the forgiveness of sins. It unites us with the Lord Jesus in his death and resurrection so that going forward we are clothed with Jesus and therefore can partake in all the spiritual benefits that come to us via the cross. The Bible says so, so why disagree.

Now, let us brief ly look at how potentially fake baptisms entered the Church. I make no apologies for referring to these practices as 'fake' and counterfeit, and you can challenge my position by entering my $30,000 Book Challenge and state your views. This is one of the points you must address biblically to win a price.

Pouring comes straight from the Didache, an ancient manuscript whose authorship remains a mystery. It has its genesis in the first or second century. Somebody appeared to have kept notes on "The Practices of the Apostles", but the identity of that somebody remains unknown. None of the Apostles in their own writings alludes to the practice of pouring as an alternative to baptism by full immersion.

The problem in dealing with pouring as a valid baptism is that even the Didache never advocated dispensing with baptism by full immersion as prescribed in the Bible. The Didache upholds baptism by full immersion. It simply tried to address a rare situation where people have heard the good news about Jesus and have believe, but there is insufficient water to baptize them. The question I believe the Didache tried to answer was: Do we let these people go home without being baptized or do we symbolically baptize them by pouring or sprinkling?

The Didache, and not the Bible, recommended that we symbolically pour water over the candidate's head three times. I deliberately highlight the term symbolically because any fool should know that anything done to symbolize something is not the real thing.

The position of the Didache was logical and practical in a situation where people have heard the word and want to be baptized, but there is insufficient water to baptize them. Pouring in this sense did not preclude the possibility that when water later became available, these people would be properly baptized. The adage 'half a *loaf is better than nothing' should* come to mind here. It was this idea that the Church subsequently adopted as its primary approach to baptism. It is quicker and involves much less effort, but is it biblical? I am afraid no.

Is this form of baptism valid in the eyes of God?

The answer should again be a clear No!

It violates the biblical standard of 'one God, one Spirit, and one baptism' that we saw in Ephesians 4:4-6. It is a man-made practice, and therefore not valid in the eyes of God. There is no evidence it brings about the same spiritual benefits of sin forgiveness and the indwelling of the Holy Spirit (Acts 2:38). It does not unite us with Jesus through baptism (Romans 6:3-4) and it does not transform us into new creations in Christ Jesus (2 Corinthians 5:17). It does not transform us into born-again Christians either (John 3:3-5).

Sprinkling as a means of cleansing us from impurities is found in several verses in the Old Testament. The practice predates Christianity. In Numbers, we find an instruction for anyone who touches a corpse to be cleansed by sprinkling water. In Ezekiel 36:25, the Bible says, *"Then I will sprinkle clean water on you, and you will be clean; I will cleanse you from all your filthiness and from all your idols."* However, the use of sprinkling as a Christian baptism is not biblical within the context of the new covenant with Jesus. In Acts 2:17-21, the Apostle Peter quoted the Prophet Joel about the arrival of the Holy Spirit. Joel 2:28-32 God did say He would pour out his Spirit on all people.

Infant baptism entered the Church in the 12th century. This is almost 1,100 years after the death of Jesus Christ. There can be little doubt this is a man-made practice. The New Testament is clear that the transformative agent that turns us into born-again Christians is found somewhere in the ritual of baptism by full immersion. That is the only baptism we find in the New Testament, the Christian Bible. It is indeed a Christian ritual and is defined as a religious or solemn ceremony consisting of a series of actions performed according to a prescribed order. It is a sequence of activities involving gestures, words, actions, or revered objects.

In the case of baptism, the ritual is prescribed by God. He did not explain why to be baptized, one must be standing in water. That is typical of all rituals. They never answer the 'why' question. All we know is that in a ritual, if we follow the prescribed steps to the letter, the intended results will follow.

What then are the possible reasons we should stand in water to be baptized? The first good reason is that this is the meaning of its Greek root 'baptizo'. It is said that the meaning of the word baptizo predates Jesus Christ by some 400 years. Some researchers say that the word is found in texts going as far back as 400 BC.

A second possible reason for one to be standing in water might be that without standing in water, your sins are not washed away; or that the devil has the power to interfere with the arrival and indwelling of the Holy Spirit if one is not standing in water. We know the devil has such powers from that passage in Daniel where the Prince of Persia was able to delay the delivery of a message from God to Daniel (Daniel 10:13). Therefore, without knowing all the elements of a ritual, we cannot vary any prescribed steps and expect the same results from performing the ritual. That is the mistake these man-made practices in baptism make.

We can also ask why these churches have chosen to disobey God on such a critical and transformative issue as baptism; that is, if they are not the proverbial wolves in sheep's clothing that Jesus warned us about. There is no argument per se that says being baptized in the manner of Jesus and the Ethiopian eunuch is harmful to your Christianity. So why do these churches continue to disobey God on baptism?

The reason might be found in the statement by the Apostle Paul that the "*Prince of this world has blinded you from the truth of Jesus Christ[35].*" Who is this Prince of this world he was talking about? He is none other than the devil himself. By being baptized the right way we are imitating Jesus in baptism and defeating the devil at the same time. In this sense, a church that does not baptize the right way should be viewed with suspicion. Are some of these churches agents of the devil as opposed to soldiers for Christ. The reason why many Christians have not been properly baptized is that the Church has brainwashed them into believing that the biblically fake baptisms of pouring, sprinkling, and infant baptism are just as valid in the God's eyes as baptism by full immersion. But why would the very people we hold in such high esteem like our clergy perpetuate a lie that denies millions of Christians entry into heaven according to John 3:3-5?

I believe sincerely that God answered that question in Mark 7:6-9 when He said "Isaiah was right when he prophesied about you hypocrites; as it is written: *"These people honor me with their lips, but their hearts are far from me. They worship me in vain; their teachings are merely human rules.' You have let go of the commands of God and are holding on to human traditions."* Since we all believe God has no reason to lie, and therefore what Jesus said in John 3:3-5 is the truth, why do we continue to disobey God on baptism? Why do we keep bearing the risk of not going to heaven when we die if it turns out God does not accept man-made church practices in baptism, when we all have access to the real thing: - baptism by full immersion?

These churches that do not baptize will not answer the one simple question most of us have, and that question is: *What will happen to all these people who have not been baptized by full immersion if it turns out God does not accept pouring, sprinkling and infant baptisms as valid baptisms?* We all have loved ones who died believing they were baptized Christians. What is their fate if I am right and the Church is wrong?

---

[35] 2 Corinthians 4:4

No one dead or alive can provide adequate answers to these questions; not even the Pope can give us an answer. Let us however give it a try. Let us join together and ask the global church, whose titular head is the Pope to answer that question. As stated before, the truth is that these post biblical fake baptisms do not baptize. By that I mean that they do not bring about the promised blessings of being in Christ once baptized. They do not wash away our sins. They do not enable us to receive the gift of the Holy Spirit; they do not unite you with Jesus Christ in his death and resurrection through baptism (Romans 6:3-4); there is no saving grace from these practices, and they do not make us born again.

Saving grace comes to us through the blood of Jesus, and Ephesians 1:7 says it best when it says, *"In him we have redemption through his blood, the forgiveness of sins, in accordance with the riches of God's grace that he lavished on us"*. But for goodness' sake, don't be a lazy reader; read the whole chapter to appreciate how saving grace is all about the blood of Jesus. To partake in all the blessings that f low from his sacrifice on the cross, one must first unite with Jesus through baptism [Romans 6:3-4].

Now that you know the truth, what are you going to do about it?

Well, this book is a call to action for all Christians affected by these man-made practices in baptism. It can help you get started on the steps you should take to be in the right standing with God. I want you to be the yeast (Matthew 13:33) that shines this light to all members of your family. You're the one who should make everything happen; the person who makes sure every member of your family who claims to be a Christian has received the one baptism of the Christian Bible.

The reality of this message is that if you hope to see grandpa and grandma in heaven again, make sure they die in Christ as opposed to dying in the church. The two are not one and the same thing. Only those baptized by full immersion can die in Christ and have that assurance that they are not barred from entering the kingdom of God. Furthermore, nowhere in the New Testament are these man-made Church practices mentioned. We therefore should dismiss all devil-inspired tricks used to mislead believers with the contempt they deserve.

Instead therefore of engaging us in a discussion about why you believe these baptisms save, I'd rather be more direct and discuss with you your reasons for avoiding a baptism by full immersion. Even the Roman Catholic Church acknowledges that baptism by full immersion is the proper way to baptize, and that it saves.

So, tell us in your own words, child of God, why have you not been baptized by full immersion. It takes only a few minutes to be baptized, and you can be baptized in your own backyard pool. All you need to do is invite a pastor and ask him/her to baptize you and your household the right way.

For those of you who have been baptized other than by full immersion, engage your pastors to explain why they pour or sprinkle water in baptism. Document their explanations, and if it does not fully rebut the points I have raised here, share it. You need to get your pastor to explain to you how you received the gift of the Holy Spirit without going through the steps prescribed in Acts 2:38. That is the scripture where God told us on Pentecost how we get the Holy Spirit to come and indwell us. I have also shown you why by baptism, the Apostle could only mean baptism by full immersion, the one baptism of the Christian Bible.

Remember that Pentecost was the first time the phenomenon of the Holy Spirit coming to indwell us happened. Now, if your own pastor will not baptize you the right way, you should explore the possibility of going to another church that baptizes. You can also invite another pastor to baptize you outside your regular church without necessarily leaving your church. Always try and invite others who have not been properly baptized like you, to join in these baptisms by full immersion. People nowadays have pool parties in summer; why not organize a baptism pool party for you and your friends as well this summer.

Ultimately, the idea is to get more and more Christians to be properly baptized. This book puts the pressure on all churches that do not baptize by full immersion to do so or justify their practices. If your pastor is adamant that other baptisms baptize as well, just like the real thing, then get them to enter our challenge and possibly win the $30,000 prize by defending their position on baptism. It's that simple.

The rules and guidelines for the Challenge are found in Appendix 1.

The End

Appendix I

The Contest
(My $30,000 Book Challenge)

The Contest is open to everyone.

You can enter either individually, as a family or as part of a group. You can get your pastor or church to help you prepare and submit a rebuttal to this narrative and **WIN** BIG!

Don't be discouraged if you cannot rebut the whole narrative, smaller prices might be made available for partial rebuttals that are valid. Bear in mind throughout that even the Catholic Church agrees that *'baptism, when properly performed in the most expressive way is by triple immersion in water'*. In your rebuttal, you should specifically address questions posed below. They are part of this Challenge.

- Is Ephesians 4:4-6 that says there is only one baptism valid scripture?
- If it is, why does the Church use more than one baptism in the Church – full immersion, pouring, sprinkling, infant baptism, to name but a few?
- If Ephesians 4:4-6 is valid scripture, which is the **'one baptism'** of the Bible? Explain your choice.
- This book has identified baptism by full immersion as the 'one baptism of the Christian Bible (Chapter 3), if you disagree, which one is that 'one baptism?
- Acts 2:38 says if we believe and are baptized, we receive the gift of the Holy Spirit. How do people **not** baptized by this one baptism, get the Holy Spirit to come and indwell them?
- If yes, how are sins washed away/forgiven other than through this **'one baptism'**?
- God says those who believe and are baptized will be saved [Mark 16:16], can anyone be saved without baptism? Explain.
- In the Great Commission, Jesus commands baptism. Have people who have been baptized by other than the **'one baptism'** of the Bible obeyed this command?
- What's your reaction to the statement 'if there is only one baptism in the Bible, any other baptisms, in addition to that 'one baptism' of the Bible must be a counterfeit'.
- Can anyone be under the new covenant with Jesus without baptism by full immersion (Matthew 28:19; Romans 6:3-4 and Colossians 2:12)? How? Explain biblically.
- By what miracle can one escape the law of Moses or other belief system without the 'one baptism' of the New Testament? (Reference Romans 6:3-4 and Galatians 3:26-27)
- Is the saving grace that comes to us via the cross available to all Christians even those **not** baptized by full immersion (reference Galatians 3:26-27)?
- Does pouring, sprinkling or infant baptism baptize, biblically?
- If you have **not** been baptized by full immersion, how do verses like Roman's 6:3-4 and Colossians 2:11-13 apply to you?

Since the practices under discussion are part of the Catholic tradition, explain paragraph 1239 of the Catechism of the Catholic Church that says:

"Baptism properly speaking. It signifies and actually brings about death to sin and entry into the life of the Most Holy Trinity through configuration of the Paschal mystery of Christ Baptism is performed in the most expressive way by triple immersion in the baptismal water. However, from ancient times it has also been able to be conferred by pouring the water three times over the candidate's head."

Baptisms other than 'triple immersion' are man-made. They include pouring, sprinkling, and infant baptism. They are potentially counterfeit (fake). Doesn't that mean these practices in baptism do not baptize in God's eyes?

Why Is This Important?

It is important because if you have not received this **'one baptism'** of the Christian Bible, it means:

You're not baptized in God's eyes (Acts 2:38), therefore,
Your sins have not been washed away (Acts 2:38)
Your sins have not been forgiven.
You do not have the Holy Spirit indwelling you (Acts 2:3)
Therefore, you're not saved (Mark 16:16)
You have not been baptized into Christ (Romans 6:3-4; Galatians 3:26-27)
You're not united with Christ through baptism (Romans 6:3-4; Colossians 2:11-13)
You have not clothed yourself with Christ through baptism (Galatians 3:26-27)
You cannot partake in any blessings that come via the cross (Romans 6:3-4; Galatians 3:26-27)
You're still under the law of Moses/or other belief system [Gal 3:13; 2:16]
You have not been redeemed by the power in the blood of Jesus (Ephesians 1:7)
You're not justified by the power in the blood of Jesus (Romans 5:9)
You're not sanctified by the blood of Jesus (1 Corinthians 6:11; Hebrews 13:12)
You're not born-again of water and the Spirit (John 3:5)
You will not go to heaven when you die (John 3:3)
You ask in vain for God to forgive your sins (1 John 1:9)
You're not In Christ, therefore you will not die 'in Christ' (Revelation 14:13)
You will not be "raptured" when Jesus returns for his church (1 Thessalonians 4:15-17)
Now, if God says there is one baptism in Christianity, help us identify it biblically.

<u>NOTE:</u>

You can change all the above in a few minutes by imitating Jesus in baptism, and as Ananias said to Saul before he became Paul, *"And now, what are you waiting for? Get up, be baptized and wash your sins away, calling on his name (Acts 22:16)."*

Be the first to submit a comprehensive rebuttal to this narrative based on the Christian Bible and WIN $30,000

105

Appendix II

(Copied From Expository Files)

The Expository Files

Faith & Baptism
Ephesians 2:8

Anyone who is saved, will be saved by grace through faith (Eph. 2:8). No principle is more fundamental to New Testament teaching, yet few principles are less understood. In the minds of many people faith stands as in isolated entity completely separate from the effect on people's lives. For this reason, it's not uncommon to see folks who really claim "faith" in Jesus, yet live like the Devil.

Real faith, is portrayed in scripture, isn't just an abstract concept that occupies one small corner of a disciple's life. Rather, one's faith is his life. His conviction is to shape every action he takes. As Paul states so eloquently, "I have been crucified with Christ; it is no longer I who live but Christ lives in me; and the life which I now live in the flesh I live by faith in the son of God, who loved me and gave Himself for me" (Gal. 2:20). To view faith apart from its effect on one's life, is to misunderstand the nature of saving faith.

If the bible's great chapter on faith, Hebrews 11, teaches us anything, it's that genuine faith is an abiding trust and confidence in God that compels one to do His will. Consider Able, Noah, Abraham, and Moses. Although none was perfect, each had a heart for God. Each one had a faith that was inextricably linked to his conduct. Real faith obeys God, and obedience serves as the only valid evidence of faith. Talk is cheap and lip-service to God is easy, as too many of us know. But changing one's life to conform to God's will, declares a faith that is genuine. It's always a mistake to sever faith and obedience.

Which brings us to our discussion of baptism. Hebrews 5:9 says of Jesus, "And having been perfected, He became the author of eternal salvation to all who obey Him." Now, can anyone rightly contend that obedience has nothing to do with salvation? Remember that faith and obedience are not mutually exclusive principles, but that they go hand in hand. What God wants is the obedience that comes from faith! (See Rom. 1:5). Any attempt at "obedience" simply for the purpose of boasting of one's works, is not Bible obedience. it is a presumptuous counterfeit. Acceptable obedience is that which is born of faith in God. And such is the nature of baptism.

On the surface of it, there is no inherent benefit from being dunked under water. Yet the apostle Peter clearly states, "The like figure whereunto even baptism doth also now save us..." (1Peter 3:21). Now if we are saved by faith as Paul says (Eph. 2:18) and if baptism is something to do with it as Peter says, then there must be some logical connection between faith and baptism.

The answer lies with Jesus. Before ascending to His Father, He instructed the apostles to "Go into all the world and preach the gospel to every creature. He who believes and is baptized will be saved; but he who does not believe will be condemned. (Mark 16:15-16). In this simple statement, Jesus links belief to baptism. At the risk of taking a passage out of context, "What God hath joined together, let not man put asunder."

Christ Commission teaches that His condition for salvation is two-fold. Belief and baptism. To omit either element is to deny the Lord's command. Belief without baptism is an empty claim without proof. And baptism without belief is a ritualistic waste of time. It's belief and baptism the Lord wants. But remember, obedience is not something "tacked on" to faith; obedience is the logical result of a faith that trusts God and takes Him at his word. No act speaks louder of our absolute faith in the grace and mercy of God, than baptism, for baptism is an act of faith. Two passages bear this out.

When some Christians in Rome felt that freedom from Mosaic Law afforded them the liberty to sin freely, Paul soundly denounced such thinking as nonsense. "What shall we say then? Shall we continue to sin that grace may abound? Certainly not! How shall we who died to sin live any longer in it?" (Rom 6:1-2). The question is, how have the saved 'died to sin?" Paul continues...

Or do you not know that as many of us as were baptized into Christ Jesus were baptized into his death?" (6:3). When did Jesus shed his saving blood for our sins? At His death when do we come in contact with his death? Paul says it's in baptism.

"Therefore, we were buried with him by baptism into death, that just as Christ was raised from the dead by the glory of the Father, even so we also should walk in newness of life." (Rom 6:4). Baptism is not a mere "sacrament" so designed by men. Neither is it a work that "earns" salvation as some seem to think. Baptism is a statement of our faith in the saving blood of Jesus Christ, and the hopelessness of being saved without it. Baptism is an act of faith that emulates the death, burial, and resurrection of Christ. But Paul teaches the same principles elsewhere in even clearer terms.

The ancient city of Colossae was noted for its influential schools of pagan philosophy and religion. Paul warns gentile Christians of the dangers of seeking some "deeper enlightenment" when, in fact, they were "complete" in Christ. (Col 2:10). They had also been subjected to the influence of Judaizers who sought to bind the Old Law, especially the right of circumcision, on gentile converts. Paul tells them they have already been circumcised spiritually – "without hands" - and have put off "the body of the sins of the flesh" (2:11). How had their sins been put off?

"Having been buried with him in baptism, in which you also were raised with him through faith in the working of God, who has raised him from the dead" (2:12). When had their sins been put off? When they were buried with Christ in baptism. Not because of the physical act itself, but because it was an expression of faith! They were "raised" with Christ through faith in God's power to raise them from spiritual death, just as He had raised His own Son from the grave. That's what baptism I – is about - not a "meritorious work" but a declaration of faith in God! And Paul explains the result of this spiritual circumcision.

"And you, being dead to your sins and the uncircumcision of your flesh, He has made alive together with Him, having forgiven you all trespasses" (2:13). It is by faith that we are saved, and that faith is declared when we submit ourselves to the emulation of Christ's death, burial, and resurrection, relying on God's power to raise us up! Any separation of faith from baptism is foreign to the Bible's teaching of salvation, and is an arbitrary distinction promoted in the theologies of men.

For one to claim faith in Jesus, yet to argue against baptism, as taught by Jesus, is incomprehensible. And to rely on the physical act of baptism alone, as a ritual rather than a statement of faith, is equally foolish. Real faith always seek to do God's will. (see Rom 3:31). Men have erected a wall of division where God never built one: between faith and obedience. Let's not further aggravate the confusion by mistakenly portraying baptism for the remission of sins is a "work," entire of itself. Instead let's speak in Bible language showing that baptism is illogical act of faith, and that baptism without faith is useless.

By Steve Dewhirst
From Expository Files 4.6;
June 1997

Appendix III

The Precious Blood of Jesus

Let us begin with Hebrews 9:22 that says, *"In fact, the law requires that nearly everything be cleansed with blood, and without the shedding of blood there is no forgiveness."* Before Jesus' supreme sacrifice on the cross, the blood of bulls and goats was used to atone for sins. The Bible says, *"For the life of a creature is in the blood, and I have given it to you to make atonement for yourselves on the altar; it is the blood that makes atonement for one's life."* (Leviticus 17:11)

But as we learn from scripture, these sacrifices failed to cleanse worshippers of their sins once and for all. Instead, they still felt guilty for their sins even after these annual sacrifices were performed. The Bible says these sacrifices were nothing but an annual reminder of sins - *"It is impossible for the blood of bulls and goats to take away sins.[36]"* It turns out God was not pleased with these sacrifices either. Then Jesus offered himself as the perfect sacrifice for sin, but to do that, God had to send him to earth in human form first. In John 3:16, God then tells us *"For God so loved the world that he gave his one and only Son, that whoever believes in him shall not perish but have eternal life."*

In John 6:51-54, Jesus himself talks about his body being the bread, and that unless we eat his flesh and drink his blood, we shall have no life in us. In taking Holy Communion therefore, Christians do so in remembrance of him.

So, what exactly does Jesus' blood do for us?

	What we get:	Explanation	Scripture
1	Forgives sins; takes away the sin of the world; becomes our atonement for sin	Sacrifice for sins; washes away our sins; propitiation for our sins	Mathews 26:28; John 1:29; Romans 3:25; Colossians 1:14; Ephesians 1:7, Hebrews 10:12; Acts 22:16; 1 John 2:2
2	Gives life (spiritual)	We eat his flesh and drink his blood	John 6:53;
3	Ushers us into the new Covent with God	Remembrance of his sacrifice on the cross; Holy Communion	1 Corinthians 11:25; Luke 22:20; Ephesians 2:12-13; Hebrews 13:20
4	Helps us remember Jesus		1 Corinthians 11:24-25];
5	Purchased the Church	With his own blood	Acts 20:28
6	Justifies us		Romans 5:9;
7	Redeems us		Ephesians 1:7; 1 Peter 1:18–19; Revelation. 5:9); Colossians 1:14

---

[36] Hebrews 10:4

8	Sanctifies us	Persistent sinning after baptism may deserve more severe punishment	Hebrews 13:12; Hebrews 10:29; Hebrews 10:10
9	Brings peace and reconciliation with God		Colossians 1:20
10	Cleanses us from all sin		Hebrew 9:14; 1 John 1:7
11	Overcomes the accuser; destroys works of the devil	Blood of the lamb and word of their testimony	Revelation 12:10–11; Hebrews 2:14; 1 John 3:8
12	Spiritually heals us	By his stripes, we are healed	I Peter 2:24; Isaiah 53:5
13	Frees us from the curse of the law		Galatians 3:13; (Galatians 5:1
14	Declares us righteous		2 Corinthians 5:21
15	Brings us into Christ		Ephesians 2:13
16	Testifies we are clean	On our behalf, washes our robes clean after "rapture"	Revelation 1:5; 7:14
17	Protects us	Passover	Exodus 12:27)
18	No condemnation	We no longer walk in the flesh	Romans 8:1
19	Brings eternal redemption	His blood more precious than that of goats and calves	Hebrews 9:12
20	Gives us confidence to enter holy places		Hebrews 10:19

END

Timeline of the Apostle Paul Crucifixion of Jesus

Paul's timeline is important. False prophets use verses from Paul's epistles to distort the message of the Bible, especially the New Testament on baptism. These epistles had not yet been written when Christianity was born (Pentecost). To accept their falsehoods on baptism is like arguing that the apostles had baptism all wrong the first 30 years of Christianity. That is the same as arguing that the apostles had baptism wrong at the beginning because they were using baptism by full immersion, when all that they needed to do was to believe in Jesus, which then would have allowed grace alone through faith to save us. These arguments are of course ridiculous, but they go to show how gullible some of our brothers and sisters in Christ are.

DATE	EVENT	BOOKS WRITTEN	OTHER COMMENTS
AD. 30	Crucifixion of Jesus/Pentecost		
AD. 32	Present at stoning of Stephen (Acts 7:58; 8:1)		
AD. 33	Persecutor of the church (Acts 8:1-3; Phil.3:6		
AD. 34	Conversion on the Road to Damascus (Acts 9:1-9)		
	Goes to Damascus (Acts 9:10-19)		
	Travels to Arabia and remains there (Gal. 1:17)		
AD. 37	Returns to Damascus, then exits the City for safety (Gal. 1:17; Acts 9:20-25; 2 Cor. 11:32-33)		
	Goes to Jerusalem (Acts 9:26-29; Gal. 1:18)		
	Goes back to Tarsus for safety (Acts 9:30)		
SD.46	Barnabas travels to Tarsus in order to seek Saul (Acts 11:25)		
AD.47	Goes to Antioch with Barnabas teaching to many people (Acts 11:26)		Disciples were called Christians for 1st time at Antioch
	Prophetess Agabus prophesies famine. Barnabas and Saul bring aid to Jerusalem (Acts 11:29-30)		
	Barnabas return to Antioch with John Mark (Acts 12:25)		
	Barnabas and Saul separated and sent out (Acts 13:2-3)		
AD. 48	BARNABAS AND Saul LEFT FOR Selicia and Cyprus (Acts 13:4)		
	While in Cyprus, they go to Salamis and Paphos (Acts 13:5-12)		
	They also go to Perga in Pamphylia where John Mark departs for home (Acts 13:13)		
AD. 48	Ministry in Antioch of Pisidia (Acts 13; 14-50)		
	At Iconium (Acts 13:51-14:6)		

	Flees to Lystra and Derbe, preaching the gospel (Acts 14:6-7)			
	In Lystra, Paul and Barnabas are mistaken for gods (Acts 14:8-18)			
	Stoned at Lystra, supposed to be dead, but re-entered the city (Acts 14:19-20)			
	Departs with Barnabas to Derbe, preaching the gospel (Acts 14:20-21)			
	Return to Lystra, Iconium and Antioch to strengthen the disciples and appoint elders (Acts 14:21-24),			
	From Pisidia, they returned to Antioch of Syria and reported their journey to the church (Acts 14:24-28)			
AD. 49	Goes up to Jerusalem with Barnabas (Acts 15:1-29); Galatians 2:1		Claudius expels Jews from Rome	
	Paul and Barnabas return to Antioch of Syria, teaching and preaching (Acts 15:30-35; Galatians 2:11-14)			
	Contention over John Mark. Barnabas and John Mark sail to Cyprus (Acts 15:36-39)			
	Paul and Silas depart, going through Syria and Cilicia, strengthening the churches (Acts 15:40-41)	Epistle to Galatians in written.9		
AD. 50	Goes to Derbe and Lystra and picks up Timothy, strengthening the churches (Acts 16:1-5)			
	They go to Traos and Paul sees a vision of a Macedonian man (Acts 16:6-10)			
AD. 51	They sail from Traos to Neapolis (Acts 16:11)			
	Then to Philippi where Paul meets Lydia (Acts 16:12-15)			
	Paul and Silas imprisoned after casting out a demon from a slave girl (Acts 16:16-25)			
	Prison doors open miraculously and the jailer saved (Acts 16:25-34)			
	Departs for Philippi (Acts 16:35-40)			
	Pass through Amphipolis and Apollonia (Acts 17:1)			
	At Thessalonica and preached Christ, but had to flee (Acts 17:1-10)			
	He leaves Silas and Timothy at Berea (Acts 17:10-14)			
	At Corinth where he is re-joined by Silas and Timothy (Acts 18:1-17)	1 Thessalonians		
AD. 52		2 Thessalonians		
AD. 53	Paul returns to Antioch after stopping at Ephesus, Caesarea, and Jerusalem (Acts 18:18-22)			
	Travels through Galatia and Phrygia strengthening the disciples (Acts 18:23)			
	Passes through the upper regions on his way to Ephesus (Acts 19:1)			

	Ministry in Ephesus (19:1-41)			
AD. 54		1 Corinthians	Claudius poisoned by his wife. Nero becomes Emperor	
AD. 56	Paul goes to Macedonia (Acts 20:1)	2 Corinthians		
	Travels to Greece (Acts 20:2)	Romans		
	Goes back to Macedonia (Acts 20:3)			
	At Traos (Acts 20:4-12)			
	Left for Assos, Mitylene, Chios, Samos (Acts 20:13-15)			
	Paul exhorts the Ephesians elders at Miletus (Acts 20:15-38)			
	To Kos, Rhodes, Patra, Phoenicia (Acts 21:1-2)			
	At Tyre (Acts 21:3-6)			
	At Ptolemais (Acts 21:7)			
	At Caesarea (Acts 21:8-14)			
AD. 57	At Jerusalem (Acts 21:15-25)			
	Paul gets arrested in the temple and causes a mob (Acts 21:26-36)			
	Addresses the mob (Acts 21:37-40; 22:21)			
	Paul's citizenship saves him from scourging (Acts 22:22-29)			
	Before the Sanhedrin (Acts 22:30-23:10)			
	Jesus tells Paul that he will bear witness of him in Rome (Acts 23:11)			
	The plot against Paul's life (Acts 23:12-22)			
	Sent safely to Felix the governor (Acts 23:23-35)			
	Paul before Felix (Acts 24:1-27)			
AD. 59	Paul before Festus (Acts 25:1-12)			
	Paul's appeal honored – turning point towards Rome (Acts 25:12)			
	Paul before Agrippa (Acts 25:13 to Acts 26:32)			
	Paul departs Rome and sails to Myra (Acts 27:1-5)			
	They sail to Fair Havens on Crete (Acts 27:6-8)			
	In spite of Paul's warning, they set sail again (Acts 27:9-12)			
	In the midst of a terrible storm, they get shipwrecked in the island of Malta (Acts 27:13 to Acts 28:1)			
	At Malta (Acts 28:2-10)			
	Sails to Syracuse (Acts 28:11-12)			
	Sails to Rhegium, then Puteoli (Acts 28:13)			
AD. 60	Arrives in Rome (Acts 28:14-16)			
	Meets with the Jews (Acts 28:17-28)			
AD. 61	Preaches the gospel without hindrance for two years in his rented house (Acts 28:30-31)	PHILEMON COLOSSIANS Ephesians		
AD. 62	Released from Roman imprisonment	Philippians 1 Timothy (62-64)		

AD. 63	Further missionary work	Titus (62-64)	
AD. 64-65		2 Timothy (c.64-66)	The Great Fire in Rome; Major persecution of Christianity begins. Josephus pleads the interests of the Jews before Rome. Nero constructs the Domus Aurea
AD. 66	Second imprisonment and martyrdom under Nero		The beginning of the Jewish Revolt against Rome
AD. 70			Destruction of the temple under Titus

END